Copyright © 2015 A.D.A. EDITA Tokyo Co., Ltd.
3-12-14 Sendagaya, Shibuya-ku, Tokyo 151-0051, Japan
All rights reserved. No part of this publication may be reproduced,
stored in a retrieval system, or transmitted, in any form or by any means,
electronic, mechanical, photocopying, recording, or otherwise,
without permission in writing from the publisher.

Copyright of photographs
©2015 GA photographers

Logotype design: Gan Hosoya

Printed and bound in Japan

ISBN 978-4-87140-583-6 C1352

# GA
Contemporary Architecture
Global Architecture

GA 13

HOUSING 1

Photographed by Yukio Futagawa

GA Contemporary Architecture 13

HOUSING 1

6	1946-52	**Le Corbusier:** Unité d'Habitation, Marseille, France ル・コルビュジエ：マルセイユのユニテ・ダビタシオン
14	1948-51	**Mies van der Rohe:** 860-880 Lake Shore Drive Apartments, Chicago, Illinois, U.S.A. ミース・ファン・デル・ローエ：860-880レイク・ショア・ドライブ・アパートメント
18	1954-59	**Hans Scharoun:** "Romeo" and "Juliet", Stuttgart, Germany ハンス・シャロウン：「ロミオ」と「ジュリエット」
22	1963-72	**Patrick Hodgkinson:** Brunswick Centre, London, U.K. パトリック・ホジキンソン：ブランズウィック・センター
26	-1973	**Hardy Holzman Pfeiffer Associates:** Cloisters Condominium, Cincinnati, Ohio, U.S.A. ハーディ・ホルツマン・ファイファー・アソシエイツ：クロイスター・コンドミニアム
30	1968-76	**James Stirling:** Town Centre Housing, Runcorn, U.K. ジェームス・スターリング：ランコーン・タウンセンター住宅団地
36	1968-76	**Fernando Higueras + Antonio Miró:** Edificio Princesa, Barcelona, Spain フェルナンド・イゲーラス＋アントニオ・ミロ：エディフィシオ・プリンセッサ
42	1969-74	**Carlo Aymonino + Aldo Rossi:** Housing Complex, Gallaratese Quarter, Milan, Italy カルロ・アイモニーノ＋アルド・ロッシ：ガララテーゼの集合住宅
52	1969-82	**Ralph Erskine:** Byker Redevelopment, Newcastle upon Tyne, U.K. ラルフ・アースキン：バイカー再開発団地
60	1970-72	**Kisho Kurokawa:** Nakagin Capsule Tower, Tokyo, Japan 黒川紀章：中銀カプセルタワービル
64	1970-75	**Ricardo Bofill / Taller de Arquitectura:** Walden 7, near Barcelona, Spain リカルド・ボフィル／タリエール・ド・アルキテクトゥラ：ウォールデン7
70	1970-76	**Lucien Kroll:** Quartier des Facultes Medicales, Brussels, Belgium ルシアン・クロール：医学部学生のための住宅団地
78	1977-81	**Manteola, Sánchez Gomez, Santos, Solsona, Viñoly:** Manantiales Housing, Punta del Este, Uruguay マンテオラ，サンチェス・ゴメス，サントス，ソルソナ，ヴィニオリ：マナンティアレス集合住宅
82	1978-82	**Arquitectonica:** The Atlantis, Miami, Florida, U.S.A. アルキテクトニカ：ザ・アトランティス
86	1978-84	**Piet Blom:** Arbres/Forêt d'Habitations, Helmond, The Netherlands ピエト・ブロム：住宅群〈木〉と〈森〉
90	1978-83	**Ricardo Bofill / Taller de Arquitectura:** Les Espaces d'Abraxas, Marne-la-Vallée, France リカルド・ボフィル／タリエール・ド・アルキテクトゥラ：アブラクサス宮殿
96	1978-99	**Tadao Ando:** Rokko Housing I, II, III, Kobe, Hyogo, Japan 安藤忠雄：六甲の集合住宅 I, II, III
106	1979-80	**A Design Group / D. Cooper, R. Clemenson, M. W. Folonis:** Barrington Condominiums, West Los Angeles, California, U.S.A. Aデザイン・グループ：バリントン・コンドミニアム
110	1980-84	**Manolo Nuñez-Yanowsky:** Les Arènes de Picasso, Marne-la-Vallée, France マノロ・ニュネズ・ヤノヴスキー：ピカソ・アリーナ
114	1982-85	**Henri Gaudin:** Housing in Evry, Evry, France アンリ・ゴーダン：エヴリーの集合住宅
118	1983-86	**Henri E. Ciriani:** Lognes, Marne-la-Vallée, France アンリ・E・シリアニ：ローニュ
122	1985-87	**Jean Nouvel:** Nemausus I, Nîmes, France ジャン・ヌヴェル：ネモジュス I
126	1988-91	**Renzo Piano:** Rue de Meaux Housing, Paris, France レンゾ・ピアノ：モー通りの集合住宅
130	1988-91	**Riken Yamamoto:** Hodakubo Housing, Kumamoto, Japan 山本理顕：熊本県営保田窪第1団地
136	1989-91	**Steven Holl:** Void Space/Hinged Space Housing, Fukuoka, Japan スティーヴン・ホール：ヴォイド・スペース／ヒンジド・スペース・ハウジング
142	1989-91	**Rem Koolhaas / OMA:** Nexus World Housing, Fukuoka, Japan レム・コールハース：ネクサスワールド・ハウジング

148	1991-96	**Frank O. Gehry:** Goldstein-Sud Housing Development, Frankfurt, Germany フランク・O・ゲーリー：ゴールドシュタイン・サウスの集合住宅
154	1992-96	**Steven Holl:** Makuhari Bay New Town, Chiba, Japan スティーヴン・ホール：幕張ベイタウン・パティオス11番街
164	1994-97	**Francis Soler**: Suite Sans Fin, Rue Emile Durkheim, Paris, France フランシス・ソレール：エミール・デュケム通りの集合住宅
168	1994-98	**Frederic Borel**: Housing Building Rue Pelleport, Paris, France フレデリック・ボレル：ペルポール通りの集合住宅
172	1994-2000	**Arata Isozaki (coordinator)—K. Sejima + A. Takahashi + C. Holy + E. Diller:** Hightown Kitagata, Gifu, Japan 磯崎新（コーディネーター）／妹島和世＋高橋晶子＋クリスティン・ホーリィ＋エリザベス・ディラー：岐阜県営住宅ハイタウン北方
180	1995-98	**Kazuhiro Kojima + Kazuko Akamatsu / CAt:** Space Block Kamishinjo, Osaka, Japan 小嶋一浩＋赤松佳珠子／CAt：スペースブロック上新庄
184	1999-2004	**Kengo Kuma:** Shinonome Apartment Building, Tokyo, Japan 隈研吾：東雲キャナルコートCODAN 3街区
188	1999-2004	**Norman Foster:** Albion Riverside Development, London, U.K. ノーマン・フォスター：アルビオン河岸再開発
192	2002-05	**BIG/Bjarke Ingels:** VM-Houses, Copenhagen, Denmark BIG／ビャルケ・インゲルス：VMハウス
198	2002-05	**Ryue Nishizawa:** Moriyama House, Tokyo, Japan 西沢立衛：森山邸
204	2002-07	**Morphosis:** Madrid Social Housing, Carabanchel, Madrid, Spain モーフォシス：マドリッド公営集合住宅
210	2003-09	**Steven Holl:** Linked Hybrid, Beijing, China スティーヴン・ホール：リンクド・ハイブリッド
216	2003-11	**Frank O. Gehry:** 8 Spruce Street (New York by Gehry), New York, New York, U.S.A. フランク・O・ゲーリー：8スプルス・ストリート（ニューヨーク・バイ・ゲーリー）
224	2004-07	**Jean Nouvel:** 40 Mercer Lodgements, New York, New York, U.S.A. ジャン・ヌヴェル：40メルサー・ロッジメント
230	2005-08	**BIG/Bjarke Ingels:** The Mountain, Copenhagen, Denmark BIG／ビャルケ・インゲルス：ザ・マウンテン
236	2005-11	**Smith-Miller + Hawkinson:** 405-427 West 53rd Street "The Dillon", New York, New York, U.S.A. スミス＝ミラー＋ホーキンソン：ウェスト53丁目405-427「ザ・ディロン」
242	2006-09	**Michael Maltzan:** New Carver Apartments, Los Angeles, California, U.S.A. マイケル・マルツァン：ニュー・カーヴァー・アパートメント
248	2007-12	**Alberto Kalach:** Reforma 27, Mexico City, México アルベルト・カラチ：レフォルマ27
254	2008-14	**Jean Nouvel:** One Central Park, Sydney, New South Wales, Australia ジャン・ヌヴェル：ワン・セントラル・パーク
260	2009-11	**SANAA:** Shakujii Apartment, Tokyo, Japan SANAA：石神井アパートメント
264	2010-13	**Kazuyo Sejima:** Kyoto Apartments (Nishinoyama House), Kyoto, Japan 妹島和世：京都の集合住宅（Nishinoyama House）

1946–52
LE CORBUSIER

UNITÉ D'HABITATION, MARSEILLE
Marseille, France

West elevation 西面

During the post-war reconstruction period, France commissioned a communal housing project to rehouse the displaced middle class. Unité d'Habitation, which was built in Marseilles, became the first of a series of new high-rise housing projects that were later built in various locations.

In 1922, Le Corbusier presented a proposal to house three million inhabitants in 'Ville Contemporaine,' a visionary plan of the modern city. The multistory housing in Ville Contemporaine suggested, as a solution to the overcrowded urban environments, a futuristic vision of the highly organized modern cities and skyscrapers. Le Corbusier continued to tackle urban problems with proposals like 'the Plan Voisin' (1925) and 'Radiant City' (1930), which were later documented in the Athens Charter in 1933. Based on his basic philosophy that cities must be functional, these proposals demanded a complete separation of functions, and to make room for both nature and humans. At the time, however, none of these proposals came to fruition. In this respect too, Unité d'Habitation is a great historical achievement.

As if a city in itself, this high-rise housing project consists of 337 apartments with 23 plan types arranged over eighteen levels of reinforced concrete, with small stores and facilities tucked into its premises. Three levels with two apartments of an L-shaped duplex connected by a shared mid-level hallway (interior street) are piled up. This arrangement allows each apartment to have both eastern and western light exposures. The living room has a double-height ceiling, creating openings of 4.8 meters on both sides of the exterior. The seventh and eighth floors are single floors with corridors sandwiched between various storefronts including the bakery, barbershop, and a post office. The seventeenth and eighteenth floors were formerly used as a kindergarten and a nursery, with a slope connecting to the rooftop garden and a small children's pool.

The facade is an assortment of precast concrete panels. The pilotis columns, railings, the rooftop elevator shafts and ventilators are all candid expressions of Le Corbusier's take on material.

This project is where many of Le Corbusier's architectural theories were put into practice. Starting with the idea of multistory housing, various elements of his proposal were realized, including the housing units based on the Modulor system, pilotis, and the rooftop garden. We continue to derive an immeasurable amount of inspiration and influence from Unité d'Habitation as one of the great prototypes of apartment housing.

East elevation 東面

South elevation 南面

Entrance on west 西側エントランス

Pilotis ピロティ

Pilotis: view toward entrance ピロティ：エントランス方向を見る

Interior street　屋内通路

Shopping street on 7th and 8th floor　商店やオフィスが並ぶ共同施設階（8，9階）

Brise-soleil on 7th floor　8階，ブリーズ・ソレイユ

Roof garden. Ventilation tower on right　屋上庭園。右は換気塔

Swimming pool and gymnasium (above)　スイミング・プールと体育室（上部）

Swimming pool (1970s)　スイミング・プール（1970年代）

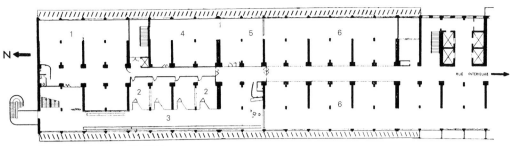
Shopping street on 7th floor

1	LOUNGE FOR HABITANTS
2	SHOP
3	CORRIDOR
4	STORAGE
5	GROCERY
6	WORKSHOP/ATELIER

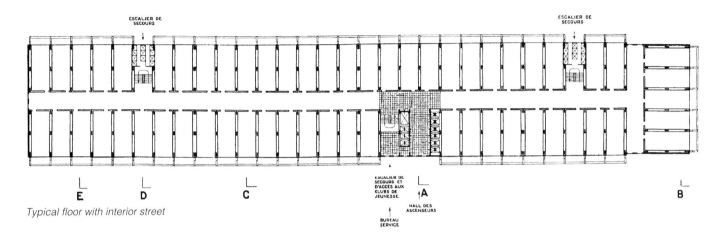
Typical floor with interior street

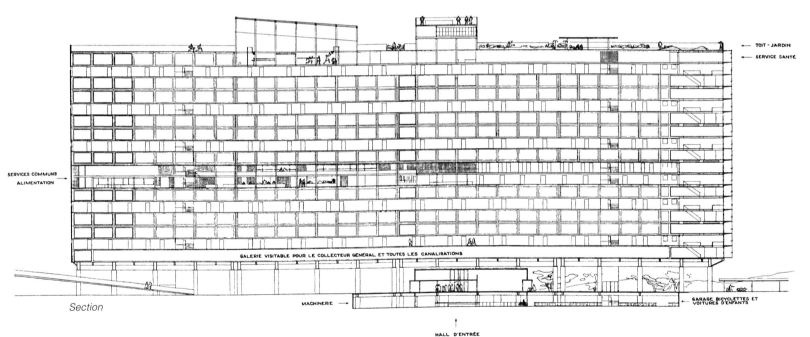
Section

戦後復興期のフランスにおいて、国家事業として中所得者層のための高層公営住宅が計画された。ユニテ・ダビタシオンと呼ばれた高層集合住宅は、このマルセイユを皮切りに、その後各地で建設されることとなる。

1922年、ル・コルビュジエは現代都市構想の一つとして「300万人の現代都市」という計画案を発表した。そこで提案された多層式住宅は、人口過密で生活環境が悪化する近代都市に対して、究極に秩序立てられ高層化する都市のビジョンが示された。その後、「パリのヴォアザン計画」（1925年）や「輝く都市」（1930年）など繰り返し都市問題に対して提唱し続け、1933年にはアテネ憲章としてまとめられた。都市は機能的であるべきだという彼の基本理念の下、自然と空間の確保、徹底した機能分離などを目指した提案は、当時いずれも実現に至ることはなかった。その意味でも、戦後を迎え、ユニテ・ダビタシオンとして実現した歴史的意義は大きい。

鉄筋コンクリート造18階建ての高層集合住宅は、23タイプ337戸の住居および小店舗や施設で構成され、さながら一つの都市をつくりあげている。基本的に1住戸は2層のL字型メゾネット式で、共用中廊下を中心に上下に組み合わせることで3層を1セットとして積層される。そのため、いずれの住戸も東西両面に採光を持つことができるようになっている。居間は2層吹き抜けになっており、4.8メートル高の開口は東西それぞれの外観にも表れている。7、8階（日本式では8、9階）のみ1層ずつの構成になっており、中廊下の両サイドには魚屋、肉屋、ベーカリー、理髪店や郵便局などの商店が並ぶ。17、18階（日本式では18、19階）には幼稚園や託児所があり（当時）、そこから屋上庭園や子供のための小さなプールを斜路が結ぶ。

外壁は、プレキャスト・コンクリートのパネルによる組み合わせである。ピロティの柱、屋上に突き出たエレベータ・シャフトや換気塔、パラペットの立ち上がりなどの造形は荒々しく、コルビュジエの素材に対する率直な表現として表れている。

ここでは、コルビュジエが唱え続けてきた多くの建築理論が反映されているといって良い。多層式住宅という提案をはじめ、モデュロール方式に基づいた居住単位、地上階のピロティ、屋上庭園などの要素がこの高層住宅において実現している。のみならず、現代に至るまで、集合住宅のプロトタイプとして与えた影響は計り知れない。

Nursery on 17th floor (1970s) 18階の託児所（1970年代）

Interior of unit: staircase to upper level
住戸ユニット内部：上階への階段

1 INTERIOR STREET
2 ENTRANCE
3 KITCHEN/ LIVING ROOM
4 MASTER BEDROOM
5 CLOSET/ SHOWER
6 BEDROOM
7 VOID

Unit plan/section

◁△ *Interior of unit: living room on lower level* 住戸ユニット内部：下階，居間

1948–51
MIES VAN DER ROHE

860-880 LAKE SHORE DRIVE APARTMENTS
Chicago, Illinois, U.S.A.

◁ Aerial view: twin towers facing on Lake Shore Drive　空撮：レイクショア・ドライブに面したツイン・タワー　　Fireproofed column　耐火被覆された柱

Entrance lobby エントランス・ロビー

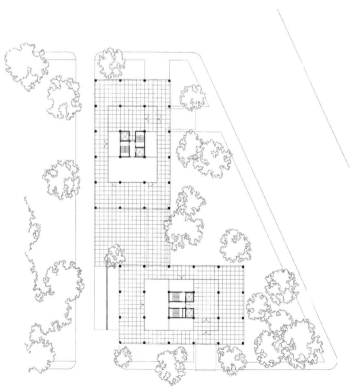

Site plan

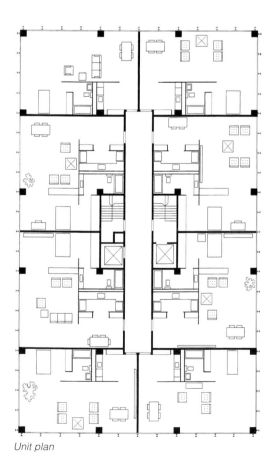

Unit plan

North up central Chicago for about 2 km, the pair of apartment buildings, standing on the site that faces Lake Michigan, are 26-story towers and is one of the representative works of Mies van der Rohe, who moved his stage of activities to the United States after the World War II. Started plotting before the war, Mies has realized glass skyscrapers as a series of 'steel and glass architecture' in the US mainly in Chicago. Here, the architectural method is proved valid also in the apartment complex building type. Used in a succession of office buildings, rationality, or a system to place a core that houses a vertical access and organize floors efficiently, is applied in these buildings as well. Residences are placed around the core and each takes in landscape that extends outside through glass walls.

The binate monolithic silhouette apartment towers were designed identically. However, one of the buildings was turned 90 degrees on the longitudinal direction and was positioned as to draw a L-shape on a travertine podium. Thus, an open space made of greenery and travertine was created on the foot of the buildings and at the same time enriches urban landscape that decorates the lakeside. The ground floor is open as a public space and residences are located on the third floor and above. Each floor height is 10 feet and the walls are composed of columns covered by fireproof steel panels and I-shape mullions that fill the gap. 8 inches by 5 1/4 inches I-shape mullions do not support vertical load and only resist wind pressure. They are rhythmically arranged in 5 feet and 3 inches intervals and glass walls are inserted between the mullions. These steel elements are painted in matt black, so as to articulately declare the orderly scale and proportion. The scenes of 'non-homogeneous' living, fitting within the frame, enhances the elevations as a whole. It is one of the prototypes of apartment complex buildings after the war.

Pilotis ピロティ

シカゴの中心部から約2キロ程北上したミシガン湖に面した敷地に建つ一対のアパートは26階建てのタワーであり、戦後アメリカに活動の舞台を移したミースの代表作の一つである。ミースは戦前に構想したガラスのスカイスクレイパーを一連の「鉄とガラスによる建築」としてシカゴを中心としたアメリカに実現しているが、この建築手法が集合住宅においても有効であることをここに証明している。一連のオフィスビルで用いられた合理性＝中心に垂直動線を収めるコアを置き、フロアを効率良く構成するシステムはここでも用いられている。住戸はコアの周りに配置され、それぞれ、外部に広がる風景をガラス壁から取り込んでいる。

一対のモノリシックなシルエットを持つアパートタワーは全く同じ建物であるが、それらの長手方向を90度ずらしてL字を描くようにトラバーチンの基壇の上に配置することで、その足元に緑とトラバーチンの広場をつくり出し、同時に湖畔を彩る都市的景観を豊かにしている。地上は共用空間として解放され、住戸群は3階以上に配置されている。それぞれの階高は10フィートであり、壁面はスティール板で耐火被覆されたコラムとその間を埋めるI型鋼のマリオンによって構成される。8インチ×5 1/4インチのI型鋼のマリオンは垂直荷重を受け持たず風圧に対するものであり、5フィート3インチのピッチでリズミカルに配置され、その間にガラス壁を構成している。これらのスティールのエレメント群はつや消しの黒色に塗装され、スケールとプロポーションの端正さを明快に表明し、これらのフレームに収まる「非均質な」暮らしの様は、総体としてこのエレベーションを豊かなものにしている。戦後集合住宅建築のプロトタイプの一つである。

1954–59
HANS SCHAROUN

"ROMEO" AND "JULIET"
Stuttgart, Germany

A pair of apartment complexes stand over a narrow piece of land, stretching from east to west. These buildings were later named by Scharoun himself as "Romeo" and "Juliet" after the famous Shakespearean play. The towers are personified with two distinctly different characteristics which are reminiscent of the male/female couple. On the eastern side stands Romeo, a twenty-storied vertical tower with elevators, staircase, and center hallway at its core. On the contrary, Juliet, which stands on the western side, is a twelve-storied low-rise. The units are placed along the circular corridor that wraps around a central courtyard with an opening towards the north.

The two towers share a unique Expressionist elevation constructed with Scharoun's usual collage-like technique, featuring various elements formed out of his dynamic palette of colors and materials. The details slightly differ, however, to amplify verticality in Romeo, and horizontality in Juliet. Each unit is equipped with a triangular porch, adding a rhythm of dynamic and structural interest. The architect's generous use of a wide palette of pale, pastel colors, and the towers' dynamic and expressive silhouettes, suggest a convergence of modernism's matured practicality and the recurring richness of the vernacular. The two towers continue to provide comfortable living to its inhabitants, with an affinity for its natural and urban contexts.

"Romeo" (right) and "Juliet" (left)　「ロミオ」(右) と「ジュリエット」(左)

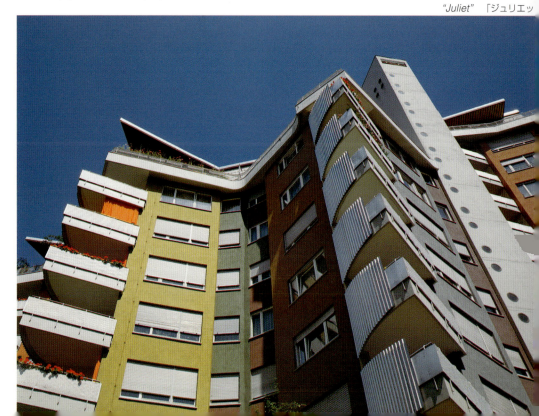

"Juliet"　「ジュリエッ

"Juliet" 「ジュリエット」

"Romeo" 「ロミオ」

"Juliet" 「ジュリエット」

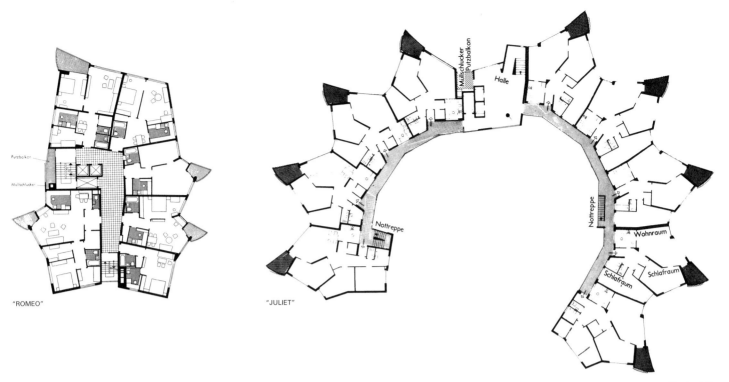

"ROMEO" "JULIET"

Typical floor

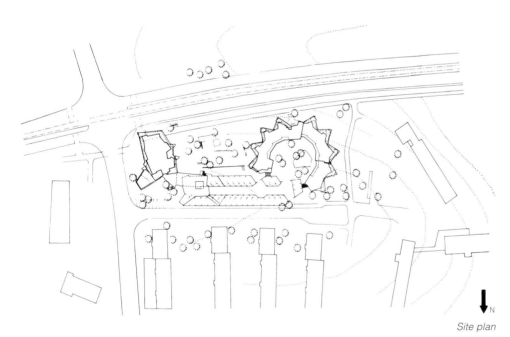

Site plan

　東西に細長い敷地に並んで建つ一対の集合住宅は，設計後にシャロウン自らによってシェークスピアの有名な戯曲から，ロミオとジュリエットとそれぞれが名付けられた。それらの姿は擬人化されたかのようでもあり，男女を想わせるような明快に異なる性格が与えられているためである。東側に配置されたロミオは20階建で，中心にエレベータや階段室のある中廊下のコアを持つ垂直性の強いタワー形式であり，それに対して西側のジュリエットは12階建の低層棟で，北側に向けて開かれた中心の円形エントランス・コートヤードを縁取るように配置された片側廊下に沿って，その外側に住戸が水平性を強調するように放射状に並べられている。

　2棟に共通する特徴的なエレベーションはシャロウンが常套した豊かな色彩と材料，それらによってつくられる形態のエレメントによるコラージュ的な手法によって独特の表現主義的な構成がなされているが，タワー棟はその垂直性を，低層棟は水平性をそれぞれ強調するようにその手法は少し異なっている。それぞれの住戸には尖った三角形平面のベランダが与えられ，それらのつくり出すリズムは，エレベーションを立体的／動的に特徴付けている。寒色から暖色まで幅の広いパステル調の淡い色彩の多用と立体的で表現的なシルエットは，成熟したモダニズムの合理性と回帰されるヴァナキュラーの豊かさの接点であり，その姿は都市や自然のコンテクストへの親和性，住民の快適性をもたらしている。

1963–72
PATRICK HODGKINSON

BRUNSWICK CENTRE
London, U.K.

View from southwest corner 南西のコーナーより見る

Brunswick Centre in London's Bloomsbury district was drawn by Sir Leslie Martin and Patrick Hodgkinson.

As it stands today, carried through by Hodgkinson who took over the project in 1963, the complex comprises 560 units of housing, 80 offices, and commercial spaces including a cinema, pubs, restaurants and services, and a garage for 925 cars.

The Centre occupies the former Foundling Hospital site partly bounded on one side by Brunswick Square and the other three primarily by low-scaled housing.

The two parallel main blocks of the Centre maintains the street line as it existed. Housing units are oriented toward the streets as well as toward the central pedestrian mall created by the main parallel blocks. Each block comprises sub-blocks of housing units which are arranged so that the perimeter block is lower in height maintaining the existing street scale, whereas the interior block is taller forming a wall to define the raised pedestrian mall. Both perimeter and interior blocks stagger toward the centre leaning against each other forming a step-back profile. This allows externally the maximum amount of light to penetrate and assures that the terraces receive maximum exposure to the sun, whereas internally, it results in a pyramidal void which in this instance is turned into a pedestrian street with open balconies for access to the living units. It is very unfortunate that this space with the heavy exposed structures reminds one of a parking garage rather than an entry to a home. Once inside, however, the typical living unit is straight forward in plan and very pleasant with the living room flooded with sunlight through a greenhouse at the end adjacent to a terrace overlooking the central pedestrian mall or the outer street depending on the location of the unit.

As the commercial street on the ground level provides enough social interaction to the neighborhood where very little commercial use existed before, and with much of the apartments occupied, the place is full of life.

View from east. Access toward plaza　東より見る。広場へのアクセス

View from plaza. Housing units above　広場より見る。上は住戸ユニット

Plaza 広場

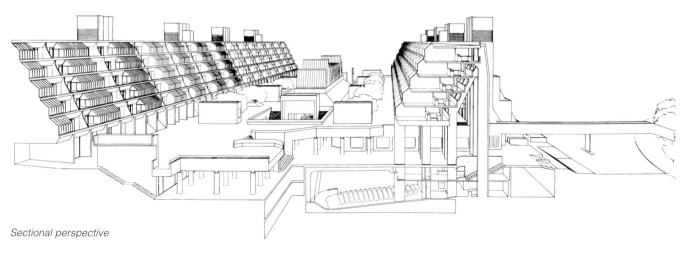

Sectional perspective

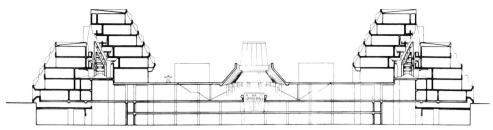
Section through housing and internal street

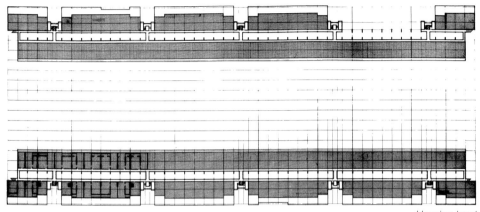
Housing level

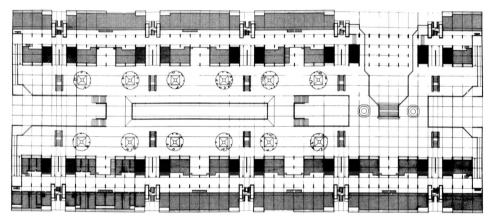
Plaza level

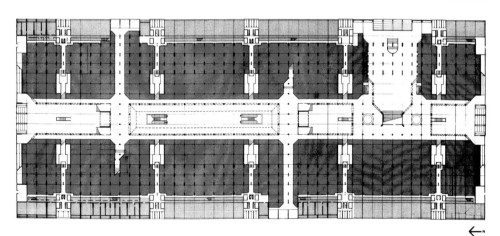
Shopping centre level

　ロンドンのブルームズベリー地区のブランズウィック・センターは，レズリー・マーティン卿とパトリック・ホジキンソンによって立案された。

　この計画は，1963年にホジキンソンが引き継ぎ，現在の状態にまでこぎつけた。現段階で，住戸は560戸，事務所80室，映画館，パブ，レストラン，各種サービス施設を含む商業スペース，925台の駐車場が完成している。

　センターの敷地は，以前，孤児院のあったところで，一方は部分的にブランズウィック・スクエアに面し，他の三方は，全般的にスケールの細かい住宅街に面している。

　センターを構成する二つのブロックは，いずれも既存の街路に対して平行に並び，住戸ユニットは，これらの街路か，二つのブロックに挟まれた中央のペデストリアン・モールのいずれかに面している。各ブロックは，二つのサブ・ブロックに分けられ，外周の街路に面したブロックは，既存の街路のスケールにあわせて高さを抑え，内側のブロックは，背を高くして巨大な壁面をつくり出すことで，地上レベルより一段上がっているペデストリアン・モールの性格を，はっきりと規定している。外周のブロックと内側のブロックは，お互いに寄り掛かるようにセットバックしている。これによって，外側では，住戸への採光とテラスへの日当りを最大限に利用し，内側では，ピラミッド形断面の空間に，各住戸へのアクセス用オープンバルコニーとペデストリアン・デッキを通すことが可能になっている。残念ながら，この内側の空間は，巨大な構造体がそのまま露出しているので，住戸への入口というよりは，駐車場のような暗い雰囲気になってしまった。しかし，一旦住戸内に入れば，各住戸ユニットはプランも極めて分り易いし，テラスの幅にとられた温室を通して，居間には自然光が一杯に注ぎ込み，極めて快適な空間がつくり出されている。テラスからは，住戸の位置に応じて，外周の街並や，中央のペデストリアン・モールを見渡すことができる。

　以前には，この近隣にほとんど商業施設というものが存在しなかったことも幸いして，現在では人も集まり，結構にぎやかな雰囲気が出来上がっている。

−1973
HARDY HOLZMAN PFEIFFER ASSOCIATES

CLOISTERS CONDOMINIUM
Cincinnati, Ohio, U.S.A.

Overall view from northeast 全景。北東より見る

"The Cloisters", so named by its owners because of the remote, secluded character of the site, is a luxury townhouse development. Designed for a high-income semi-retired market, the project contains typical two-bedroom units with large spaces similar to those that tenants previously enjoyed in their suburban homes.

Location
Situated on a precipitous site on the southern slope of Mount Adams, it enjoys a panoramic view of the Ohio River and the Kentucky countryside beyond. A prerequisite of the project was to ensure that each living unit would have an unobstructed access to this view. Close to downtown Cincinnati and located in a neighborhood reminiscent of a European hillside town, "The Cloisters" is attractive to its tenants and a success for its owners.

Solution
Two basically different site characteristics and the need to provide parking for two cars for each unit led to the development of two typical unit plans. (Although a luxury project, the necessity for repetitive unit plans cannot be overlooked in light of the savings and ease of construction.)

A Units
The typical A units are provided with angular window projections which take maximum advantage of the view, at the same time altering the configuration of an otherwise rectangular living environment. To provide variety and to give each unit an individual character, every other typical unit plan is reversed, with windows occurring in different places on each unit. In addition, the roofs of adjacent projections pitch in opposite directions, and the balconies overhead are placed in different locations, thus further altering the space below.

B Units
The typical B units, because of their orientation to the site, have no angular window projections but the alternating location of the balconies above is used to give variety to the living areas below.

In the A and B units, bedrooms, bathrooms, kitchens, and storage areas have been pro-

View toward B units over courtyard 中庭越しにB型ユニットを見る

View toward B units from northeast 北東よりB型ユニットを見る

vided in a traditional manner, insuring only that they contain the amount of space and quality previously available in most of the tenants' homes.

The remaining spaces—living, dining, and entertaining areas—are left open to allow for maximum flexibility of movement and furniture placement. Both A and B units are additionally provided with outdoor balcony spaces, while the B units also have access to gardens below.

Planning
A grouping of two-story typical A units with garage spaces beneath is located at the top, flat portion of the site, while the two-story typical B units step down the hillside and out of view of the others. At the intersection of these two L-shaped configurations non-typical spaces are formed which were custom designed at the request of specific clients. An inclined elevator connects the hillside B units with the parking area above.

Structure and Finish Materials
The entire wood frame construction of the project is supported on the sloping site with telephone poles, eliminating the necessity for massive foundation walls and costly excavation of slabs on grade. The exterior of the building is sheathed in vertical 1 x 4 boards and the major roof areas are covered with terra cotta tiles.

The masonry party walls, providing fire separation between every two units, are left exposed and, with oak boards and painted plaster, form the major interior wall surfaces. Tile, stone, and oak boards are used for floor areas throughout. Built-in metal fireplaces, kitchen cabinets and appliances, and other miscellaneous interior design choices are available at each tenant's option.

Future Expansion
Because of its repetitive configuration, "The Cloisters" will be able to grow without compromise in both northerly and westerly directions as more property is acquired. This will allow yet other tenants to enjoy a living environment with a panoramic view of the countryside.

View toward Ohio River through pathway of B units B型ユニットのデッキ越しにオハイオ川を望む

View from southeast. A units (left) and B units (right) 南東より見る。A型ユニット（左）とB型ユニット（右）

Pathway between units. Elevator on center 住戸間のデッキ。中央はエレベータ

敷地が、閑静で人里離れた土地にあるというので「ザ・クロイスター」と名付けられたこの計画は、ぜいたくなタウンハウス開発計画である。このタウンハウスは、収入が多く、半ば引退した高年層を対象に計画されており、典型的な2寝室型住戸からなっている。各住戸は、対象とされた人々が以前住んでいた郊外住宅と同じ程度のゆったりしたスペースが確保されている。

敷地：
敷地は、アダムス山の南向き斜面にあり、かなり勾配はきついが、オハイオ川やケンタッキーの村々のすばらしい景色が眼前に繰り広げられている。計画のポイントは、この眺望を妨げずに、各住戸にいかにアクセスするかということであった。「ザ・クロイスター」は、シンシナティの繁華街に近く、まわりは、ヨーロッパの郊外住宅地を彷彿とさせる場所柄である。利用者にとっては、魅力あふれる計画であり、所有者にとっては、成功した企画ということができよう。

方法：
敷地が二つの基本的に異なった性格を持つこと、各々の住戸に2台の駐車スペースを確保する必要のあることから、この開発計画の住戸プランは2タイプとなった（高級分譲住宅ではあるが、工事のしやすさと、工費節減の見地から、住戸のある程度の規格化は避けられなかった）。

Aタイプ住戸：
Aタイプ住戸には、直角に突き出た窓がある。これによって、眺望を最大限に楽しむことができる。同時に、他の矩形の平面レイアウトに変化を引き起こす要素となっている。各々の住戸単位に変化と個性を与えるため、一つおきに単位が繰り返されており、窓は各住戸ごとに開口部の位置が違う。その上隣り合う出窓の屋根はそれぞれ反対方向に勾配が付いており、上階のバルコニーは違った場所に取り付けられている。当然、下の空間は、それ以上に変化に富むこととなった。

Bタイプ住戸：
Bタイプの住戸は、敷地の方位の関係で直角に突き出た窓はないが、上階のバルコニーの位置を変えることによって、下階の居住空間に変化をもたらすことが可能となった。

A、Bタイプとも、寝室、浴室、厨房、収納スペースは、従来通り用意されているが、それぞれのスペースのゆとりや、内容は、これらの住居に住む人々が以前使用していたものと同等以上のものを備えている。

居間、食堂、遊戯室などその他のスペースは、人の動きや家具のレイアウトのフレキシビリティを充分確保できるようオープンのままになっている。Aタイプ、Bタイプ住戸とも、屋外のバルコニーが用意されるが、Bタイプ住戸からは下の庭に降りることもできる。

全体計画：
下階にガレージを有する2層のAタイプ住居群は、敷地の一番上の平らな部分に配置されている。一方、2層のBタイプ住戸は、斜面に沿って配置され、下の住戸は上の住戸の視野を妨げないように計画されている。これら二つの住戸群が接する場所には、二つのニュートラルなL字形のスペースができ、これらは、クライアントのリクエストにより個別に設計がなされた。斜面に建つBタイプ住戸は、上にある駐車場とは、斜面に沿って動くエレベータで結ばれている。

構造と仕上げ：
斜面に建つ木構造の住戸はすべて電柱に使われる丸太材によって支持されており、大きな基礎やコストのかかる急斜面での根切りは省略された。建物の外壁は、1×4インチ板材の竪羽目張りで、主屋根部分はテラコッタの瓦で覆われている。

住戸間の防火壁としてつくられたレンガ積の壁はむき出しのままでインテリアの要素となっており、他の壁面は主にオーク板張り、プラスター塗で仕上げられている。床材としては、タイル、石、オークが全体に使用されている。ビルト・イン式の金属製暖炉、厨房セット、その他の備品、インテリア・デザイン等は、それぞれ住み手のオプションでとりそろえることができる。

将来の増築計画：
一つの形を繰り返しているので、「ザ・クロイスター」は、もし土地が得られさえすれば、北へも西の方へも成長することができる。その上、増築後の入居者も、郊外の開けたすばらしい眺めを生活の中で充分楽しむことができるであろう。

Courtyard on right.
B units (left) and A units (center)
右は中庭。B型ユニット（左）とA型ユニット（正面）

Interior of B unit　B型ユニット内部

Interior of A unit　A型ユニット内部

Interior of B unit　B型ユニット内部

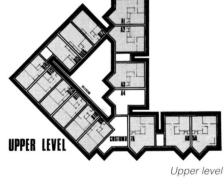

Upper level

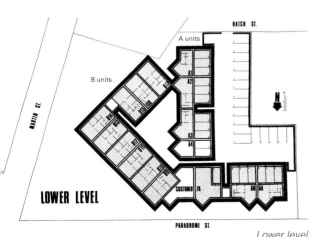

Lower level

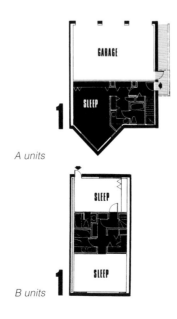

A units

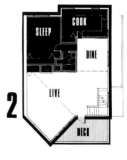

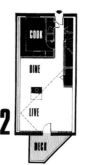

B units

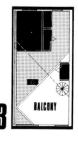

1968–76
JAMES STIRLING

TOWN CENTRE HOUSING
Runcorn, U.K.

Elevation facing garden square 庭側の壁面

The new town of Runcorn is sited mid-way between Liverpool and Manchester and a primary intention was to relieve unemployment, particularly in Liverpool, and provide an alternative to living in the 19th Century slum housing which still exists in large areas of Liverpool and Manchester.

The financing of the New Towns is through the Central Government in London and low cost housing is rigidly maintained at a minimum via the stringency of Ministry of Housing Cost Yardsticks. The Corporation and advisors of the New Town compiled the brief relating to density, site, family structure, car ownership etc.

The construction of the town centre housing (approx. 6,000 people) has commenced on land immediately south of the Town Centre building of which the first stage has been completed in 1976. All residents are within two to five minutes walk of the Town Centre and there are 1,500 dwellings (117 persons per acre) in the new housing community.

Family structure is approximately: one third 2 and 3 person flats, one third 4 person maisonettes and one third 5 and 6 person houses. This ratio of family sizes is dispersed evenly to avoid concentration of any particular social group in any part. The varieties of dwelling types are contained within a building of five stories which at ground level also include garages. The living areas of the 5 and 6 person family houses are at ground level with an outside private garden; bedrooms are on the floor above. At second floor and entered from high level pedestrian footways, are the 4 person maisonettes with living areas at the lower level related to an outdoor terrace; bedrooms are on the floor above. At the upper level of the building are single floor flats for 2 and 3 persons. Habitable rooms all face south, west or east and all dwellings are to Parker Morris size and heated from a District Heating Plant that also serves the Town Centre Building.

The terraces of housing form a series of residential garden squares that vary in size and also degree of enclosure and outlook (the outdoor rooms of the city; the idea of Bath, Edinburgh, etc.). All are tree planted and landscaped and contain children's play areas and

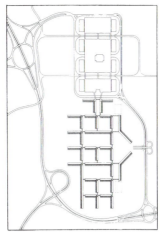
Housing

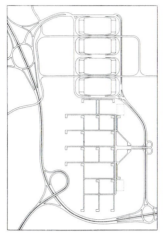
Vehicular

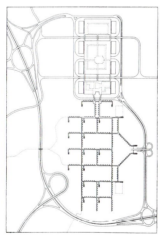
Pedestrian

Elevation facing street　敷地内の道路側壁面

the larger squares have tennis courts. These garden squares are for the use of the families which live around them and entry is either off the access road or via a pedestrian ramp which rises from the square, to connect with public footways at second floor level. These ramps can also be used for furniture removal, milk floats, refuse collection, and they allow movement of prams and pushchairs into the garden squares.

On two sides of the squares are access roads (cul-de-sacs) for residents' cars which allow entry to garages within the terraces and also to visitor's layby parking. The requirement was for 1.5 car parking spaces per dwelling, the 0.5 being for visitors and with this arrangement cars are not likely to be parked more than 30' 0" horizontally from the drivers' dwelling.

Pedestrians using the elevated footways are connected by bridges to the Town Centre building at the main level of shopping and entertainments (multi-level car parks under). These walkways are continued south and west out of the site to link with adjoining housing areas. Owing to the proximity of the Town Centre and its large number of facilities, there was only minor requirement for public houses (2) and shops (2) and these are located in the small open areas at the junction of the 'L' shaped terraces. However, as each square has a similar small space there is provision for accommodating future unforeseen requirements. (Already a laundry and a chapel have been requested). An industrialized method of construction (heavy pre-cast concrete structural walls) was developed to allow maximum off site fabrication. The nonstructural walls flanking the pedestrian footways, where there is close tactile contact, are of GRP (Glass Reinforced Polyester) in differing color combinations related to the identity of particular squares.

James Stirling

View from garden square　庭より見る

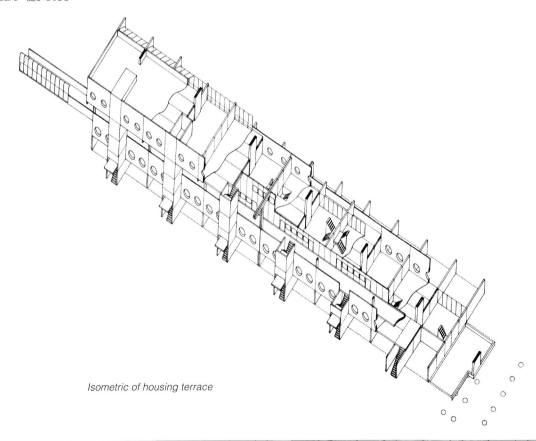
Isometric of housing terrace

Elevation

　ランコーン・ニュータウンは，リヴァプールとマンチェスターとのちょうど中間にある。建設の主な目的は，特にリヴァプールにおける失業対策事業である点と，もう一つはいまだにリヴァプールとマンチェスター両市の大部分を占めている19世紀のスラムからの住替地の提供，という2点であった。

　ニュータウンの建設費は，ロンドンの中央政府が調達するので，住宅省の定めるコスト基準にもとづいて，予算は必要最小限のコストに抑えられている。さらに，人口密度，敷地，家族構成，自家用車の所有率などの条件も，ニュータウン公社と政府顧問によって設定されていた。

　タウンセンター住宅団地（計画人口約6,000人）の建設は，タウンセンターの建物の真南に接する場所から開始された。このタウンセンターは，その第1期工事が1976年に完成している。

　ここの住民は，すべてタウンセンターまで歩いて2分から5分の距離内に住み，新しいコミュニティの規模は，1,500戸（エーカー当り117人）である。

　家族構成は，大体以下のように計画された。2人から3人家族用のワン・フロア住戸が全戸の3分の1，4人家族用メゾネット住戸も3分の1，5人から6人家族用住戸も3分の1である。こうした家族人数の割合は，特定の社会層が一個所に偏って集中しないように，全体に渡って均一に分散させた。この3種類の住戸タイプは，地上レベルにガレージを持つ，5階建の一つの建物の中に収められている。5〜6人家族用住戸のリビング・エリアは1階にあり，その外には各戸専用の

Partial elevation of stepped terraces　ずれながら重なるテラス

Footway on upper level 上階，通路

Partial elevation on street. Garage on ground level, stair tower leading to footway and units on upper floors
道路側壁面。1階は車庫。階段のタワーは上階の通路と住戸へのアクセスとなる

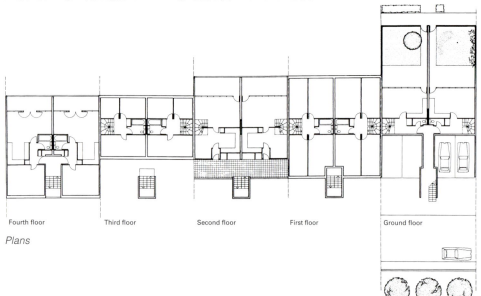

Fourth floor　　Third floor　　Second floor　　First floor　　Ground floor

Plans

Corner 角部

庭を取っている。この住戸の寝室は2階にある。3階には，ペデストリアン・デッキからの入口を持った4人家族用のメゾネット住戸があり，3階にリビング・エリアと屋外テラス，4階に寝室が置かれている。建物の最上階（5階）は，2～3人家族用のワン・フロア住戸である。居室はすべて，南，西，東のいずれかに面しており，住戸の面積は，すべてパーカー・モリス報告の基準値に適合している。各住戸はタウンセンターと共用の地域暖房プラントによって暖房している。

テラス住戸を連続させることによって，大きさ，囲い込みの度合，見晴らしなどが各々異なった，様々な庭園広場が形づくられる。（これは，いわば都市における戸外の部屋とでも言うべきものであり，バースやエジンバラなどの広場の考え方に通じるものである）。広場は，すべて植樹と各種の修景が施され，子供の遊び場や，大きな広場には，テニスコートなどが置かれている。広場は各々，それを取り囲んで住む家族が使用し，入口はアクセス道路からの脇道と，3階レベルのペデストリアン・デッキから広場に通じる斜路の，二通りがある。この斜路は，広場への入口のほかに，家具の移動，ミルクの運搬，ごみ収集などにも使えるし，乳母車や車椅子でも，広場に入ることができる。

アクセス用自動車道路（クル・ド・サック方式）は，広場を囲む2面に添って通り，住民の車はここから，建物内のガレージに入るか，来客用の道路脇駐車場に駐車することになる。駐車台数は，1戸あたり1.5台，及び1戸あたり0.5台の来客用駐車場，という要求条件であった。この配分で計画すれば，各住戸から30フィート以内に駐車できる計算である。

歩行者は，ペデストリアン・デッキを通り，ブリッジを渡って，タウンセンター内のショッピングセンターや娯楽施設に行くことができる（これらの施設の下は，立体駐車場になっている）。

このペデストリアン・デッキは，さらに南と西に延びて，隣接する住宅地域へ達している。タウンセンターが極めて近い距離にあり，センター内に十分な施設が収められているので，パブや小売店舗は，それほど必要がなかった（現在は，各々2ヶ所ずつ置かれている）。これらは，住棟がL型に曲がる部分の小さなオープン・スペースに置かれている。しかし，広場の角にはすべて同じような部分があるので，将来何らかの施設が必要になれば，この場所に設置することで対応できる（既に，クリーニング店と教会が要求されている）。

現場工事をできるだけなくするために，（プレキャストのコンクリート大型パネルによる）工業化工法が開発された。ペデストリアン・デッキに添った非耐力壁は，直接人間に触れる部分でもあるため，GRP（ガラス繊維強化ポリエステル）のパネルを使用し，色の組み合わせを，様々に変えることによって，それに面する広場の性格付けを行っている。

（ジェームス・スターリング）

Elevated footway connecting each wing and Town center
ペデストリアン・デッキは各棟やタウンセンターをつなぐ

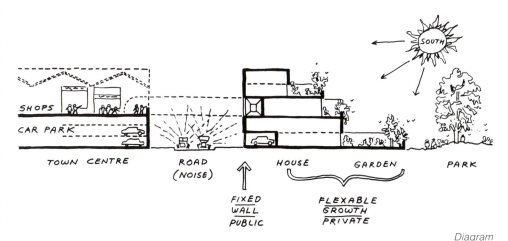

Diagram

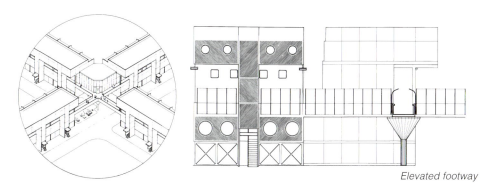

Elevated footway

1968-76
FERNANDO HIGUERAS + ANTONIO MIRÓ

EDIFICIO PRINCESA
Barcelona, Spain

A wing (right), B wing (left) and C wing (center beyond)　A棟（右），B棟（左），C棟（中央奥）

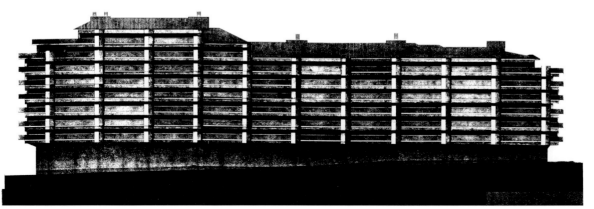

A wing: north elevation　S=1:800

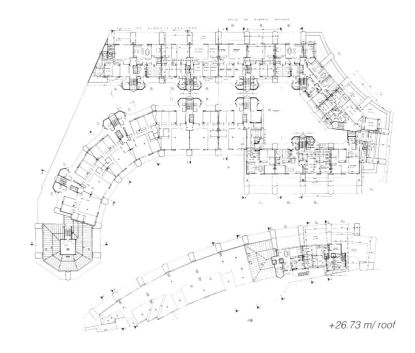

+26.73 m/ roof

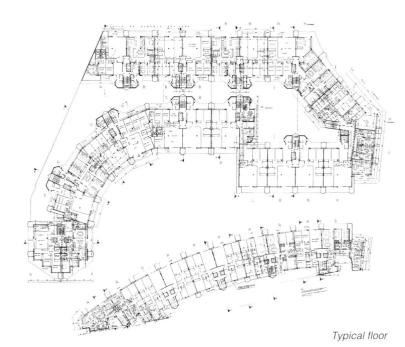

Typical floor

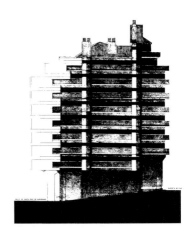

C wing: east elevation

C wing: northeast elevation

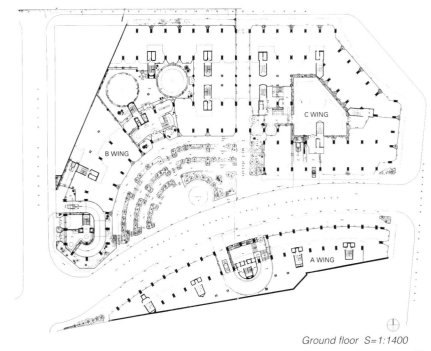

Ground floor S=1:1400

B wing　B棟

B wing: entrance B棟エントランス

View from A wing toward C wing A棟よりC棟を見る

B wing: ceiling of entrance hall
B棟：エントランス・ホール天井

C wing: courtyard　C棟：中庭

C wing: entrance hall　C棟：エントランス・ホール

Location is a 13,000 m² plot on the corner of San Bernardo and Alberto Aguilera streets. This is an important traffic intersection in the San Bernardo plaza, and the building edge would have to follow the circular outline of the plaza. A building at the northwest corner of the plot keeps the building from having facades opening onto all four sides.

Adapting to the environment
By continuous-line construction with the same heights, sightlines and offsets as the old buildings in the area.

Layout
A block of housing units for army chiefs and officers with formats and floor space rangins from 90 to 240 gross constructed square meters. A continuous line of construction with all of the housing units looking out on two sides and paired about the vertical communication cores. Basements 2 and 3 are for underground parking and basement 1, the ground and the first floor are for storefronts and businesses. Only four main entries interrupt the large ground floor area set aside almost completely for businesses. These four entries lead to inner streets on the first floor which lead to the vertical housing unit access cores.

Construction
Structure and enclosures of white concrete poured on site combined with vertical panels also prefabricated on site on non-structural parts of the facade. The vertical structural elements are columns of 1.50 x 0.80 meters, 14 meters high, with 9-meter passages in basements and business areas. Where the housing unit floor start these pillars or columns widen, forming bracket capitals which gather the pillars set 4.5 meters apart which form the conventional structure of the upper stories. All of the facades, both exterior and interior, have long, flying terraces across the front. These terraces are landscaped and protect from the sun in summer and from the rains in winter. The terraces of one apartment are separated from the next by enormous planters the lower part of which houses the electric illumination of the lower planter. The openings in the facades are treated with sliding aluminum doors and windows and roll-up plastic shades of the same color as the concrete. These openings conceal the bearing beams which run along all of the facades at a uniform distance from the ground of 2.10 meters. This makes all of the doors and windows the same height.

Special and design aspects
An attempt was made to use as few different materials as possible: white reinforced concrete in the structure and the facades with plastic shades of the same color in order to act as a monochromatic backdrop for the garden planned along the facades.

Upward view of B and C wing
B棟とC棟，見上げ

Upward view from parking on basement (B wing)
B棟，地下パーキングより見上げる

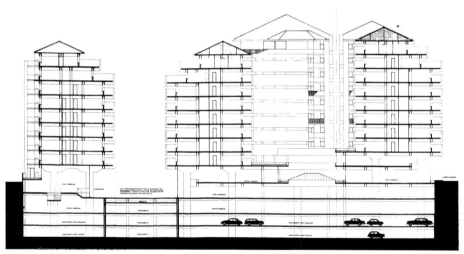
Section through A-C wing S=1:800

サン・ベルナルド通りとアルベルト・アグィレラ通りの角地に位置する13,000平米の区画である。ここはサン・ベルナルド広場の交差点として交通上重要であり，建物の側面は広場の外周に沿ってカーブさせなければならない。敷地の北西部分の建物は4方向すべてが，通りに面したファサードを有している。

環境への適応
これは，この地区の古い建物にみられるような同一高度，外観線およびセットバックを考慮したリニア状の構成である。

レイアウト
陸軍の将校や士官のための住居ユニットブロックで，各種タイプがあり，総床面積90〜240平米のものが並ぶ。住居ユニットは，連続的に並列した構成である。2方向に開かれ，垂直コミュニケーション・コアをはさんで対に配置されている。地下2，3階は駐車場，地下1階および地上1，2階は店舗と事務所である。ほとんどを事務所用のスペースにあてられている広々とした1階のフロアをさえぎるのは，わずかに四つのメインの入口だけである。これらの四つの入口は，住居ユニットへの垂直コアへ続く2階の内部通路へと導く。

建設
現場打ちコンクリートの骨組と壁体は，ファサードの非構造要素である，現場でプレハブ化した垂直パネルと組合わされる。垂直の構造要素は地下と事務所部分では，高さ14メートル，柱間9メートル，断面1.5×0.8メートルの柱である。それらの柱が広くなる部分より住居階は始まる。それらの柱は，各階とも同じ型の構造体を形成するために，4.5メートル間隔に置かれた柱を集めたブラケット状の柱頭を持つ。すべてのファサードは，外側と内側に正面を横切るキャンチレバーのテラスの連なりを有する。それらのテラスには花壇が置かれ，夏の日差し，冬の雨を防ぐことになる。この住居のテラスは，さらに大きな花壇によって隣りのテラスより仕切られ，この花壇の下部には下の花壇を照らす照明設備が組み込まれている。ファサードの開口部はアルミニウムの引き戸と窓と，コンクリートと同色のプラスチック製の巻き上げ式のブラインドからできている。これらの開口部は床より一率2.1メートルの高さで，全ファサードを走る梁に組み込まれる。これはすべての扉や窓を同一高さに揃える。

特記
できるかぎり材料の種類を少なくすることが考えられた。例えば，ファサードに沿う庭園のためモノクロームの背景を必要とすることから，構造体は白色鉄筋コンクリート，そして同色のプラスチックのブラインドを施した。

1969–74
CARLO AYMONINO + ALDO ROSSI

HOUSING COMPLEX, GALLARATESE QUARTER
Milan, Italy

Rossi's D block on left and Aymonino's B block on right　左にロッシのD棟，右にアイモニーノのB棟

Overall view from southwest. A1 (left) and A2 (right) blocks by Carlo Aymonino　南西側全景。Ａ１棟（左）とＡ２棟（右）はカルロ・アイモニーノによる設計

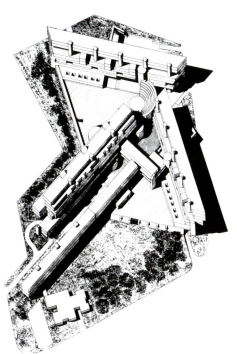

Isometric

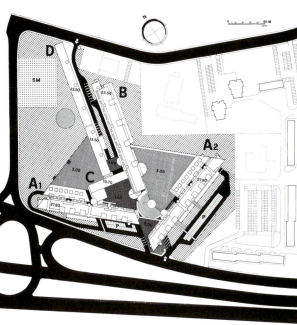

A1, A2, B　Carlo Aymonino
D　Aldo Rossi

Site plan　S=1:5000

In the green belt on the north-west limits of the city of Milan and on the edges of the largest post-war residential quarter—"Gallaratese"—one finds three building blocks arranged along a rhomboid-shaped platform: two lie along adjoining sides, the other along the diagonal. A fourth, somewhat lower block, designed by Aldo Rossi, runs parallel to the latter. This building block, property of the City of Milan which has allocated it for residences for its employees, houses something like 2,400 people.

For Italian architecture these buildings represent the end-product of a certain kind of study in housing typology and urban morphology initiated in the early '60s by Aymonino and Rossi at the School of Architecture in Venice. They also indicate that we are now entering a new phase. Thanks to this common theoretical base the structures, side by side, emphasize the opposite outcomes of that research work. At the same time they are a demonstration of the intelligence of their authors insofar as they confirm the gap existing between theoretical analysis and planning on the one hand and a striking instance of the arbitrary nature of the architectonic sign on the other.

Red plaster, which gives a monolithic tone to the whole and is interrupted only by the yellow of the foot-bridge and the blue of the corridors, makes a striking contrast with the white plaster of Rossi's long railing.

Aymonino concentrates and accumulates all the materials of his architecture—simple geometrical figures and their broken-down versions, walks, urban relations, and the complex section. A whole range of residential models—courtyard, duplex flats on the upper floors (passing through the gallery-like organization of the middle floors)—has been applied in the complex stepped section, out of which the big cylinders of the lifts protrude at regular intervals. It almost looks like an attempt to rise out of the scale of the normal building into that of the "macrostructure": a confusion of "materials" attenuated by the simplicity and homogeneity of the "matter". Counterbalancing the tempered tumult of Aymonino's experiment is Rossi's high gallery, marked by serried ranks of septa and dominated by a long wall perforated at regular intervals by the square windows of the flats.

A sharp crack parallel to the point of dilation splits the long block into two parts, supported at that point by four enormous cylindrical pillars rising before the big flight of stairs leading up to the arcade on the next floor.

Here the type of linear porticoed house is offered axiomatically as a typology. However, the split serves to indicate the repetition of the process of composition and break-up which underlies the apparent fixity of Rossi's work.

Perhaps here at "Gallaratese II" the old rivalries of the '50s between Roman organicism and Milanese Rational Architecture will finally make way for the disenchanted embrace of an "historical compromise".
Pierluigi Nicolin

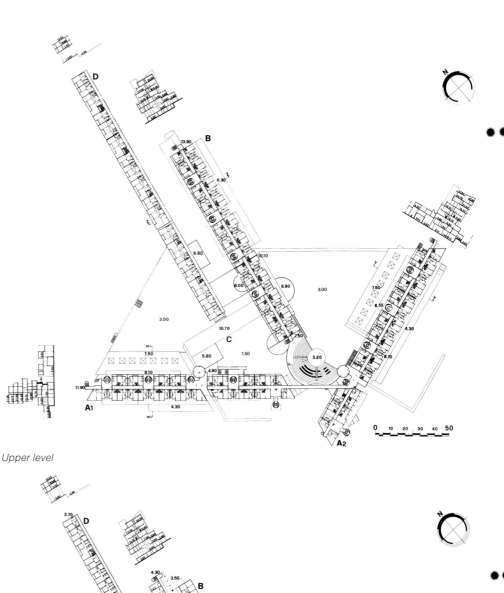
Upper level

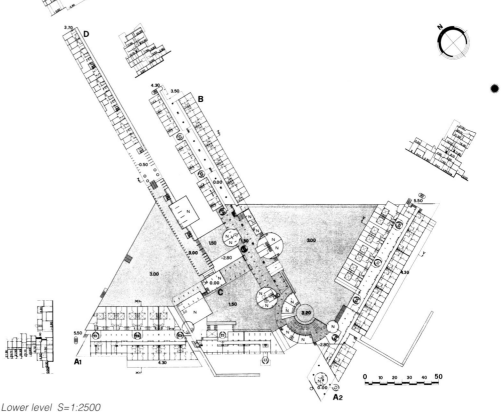
Lower level S=1:2500

A1, A2, B Carlo Aymonino
D   Aldo Rossi

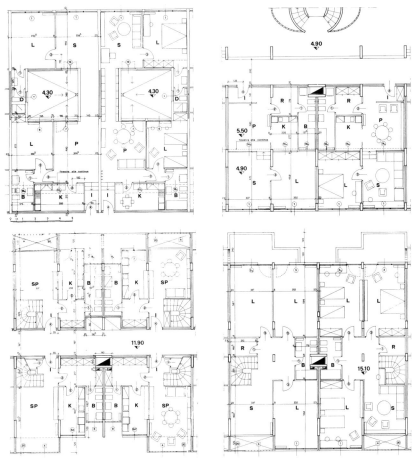

A1, A2, B blocks typical plan S=1:600

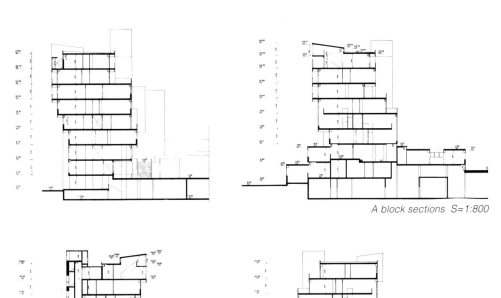

A block sections S=1:800

B block sections

ミラノの市域の北西の境界となるグリーン・ベルトのなか，戦後建設された最大の団地「ガララテーゼ」のへりの方に，菱形の基壇を築いて三つの棟が建っている。そのうち2棟は山型に互いの側面を突き合わせ，もう1棟が菱形の対角線方向に延びている。さらにアルド・ロッシの設計した第4の棟は，やや他よりも丈が低く，後者と並んで建っている。

この一群の建物は，現在ではミラノ市の職員住宅となっており，約2,400人の人々が住んでいる。

イタリア建築の歴史から見た場合，この建物はヴェネツィアの建築学部でアイモニーノとロッシが1960年代のはじめに推進した建築および都市の形態についての研究の到達点を示すものであり，建築の新しい相の幕開けを告げる存在である。この共通の理論的基盤のおかげで，ここに並び立った建物にはこの研究から導き出される成果の異なった側面があざやかに浮かび出ている。それはまた同時にそれをつくった人々の知性の証しでもあり，彼らが，記号としての建築が示すまったくの自在さと理論的探求や計画とのあいだに存在するずれをよく承知していることを示している。

アイモニーノの建物ではブリッジの黄と廊下の青を除いてすべて赤のプラスターが吹付けられており，それはマッスの単一性を強調するとともに，ロッシの横長の棟の白のプラスター仕上げと良い対比を見せている。

アイモニーノは，単純な幾何学的形態とその断片，通路，取りつき部分，複雑な断面形といったその建築のいっさいの要素を凝集させ一つに積み重ねた。1階の庭付きのユニットから上階のメゾネット・タイプのもの（その中間にギャラリーのような構成がはさまれる）にいたるまで，いっさいの住戸は複雑な段状の断面に構成され，それを突き破ってエレベータの巨大な円筒形のシャフトが一定の間隔をおいて立ち上がる。そのさまは，さながら普通一般の建築の尺度を抜け出して〈大架構〉を求める試みとも見えるほどである。こうしてさまざまな〈構成要素〉が示す喧噪は，〈テーマ〉の示す単純と均質によって中和されるのである。

いっぽう背の高い柱廊のあるロッシの棟では，ちょうどこのアイモニーノの実験の抑制された喧噪とは対照的に，壁柱が細かくリズムを刻み，四角い窓が規則正しくうがたれた長大な壁が全体を支配している。

棟の延びていく方向と直角に走る鋭い裂け目は長い棟を二つの単位に切断するが，建物はその部分で4本の大きな円柱に支えられており，その柱の群がさらに上のレベルの柱廊へと導く大階段への導入部の役割を果している。

ここでは片廊下型の住宅型式の直截な表現が求められているが，そのなかでこの裂け目はロッシの作品の基調をなす複合と切断の交錯の手法をよく示すものとなっている。

おそらくこのガララテーゼにおいて，1950年代におけるローマの有機主義とミラノの合理主義とのあいだのかつての対立が，いつの日か新鮮な想いで相抱擁する日に向けての〈歴史的妥協〉の道を歩みはじめたのである。

（ピエルルイジ・ニコリン）

View toward A2 block over outdoor amphitheater 屋外円形劇場越しにA2棟を見る

Carlo Aymonino Block

Colorful corridor through B block on ground floor 原色で彩られたB棟1階通路

View of corridor on typical floor 基準階の廊下

Pedestrian ramp on southwest facade of A1 block seen from south　A1棟南西面の斜路を南より見る

Aldo Rossi Block

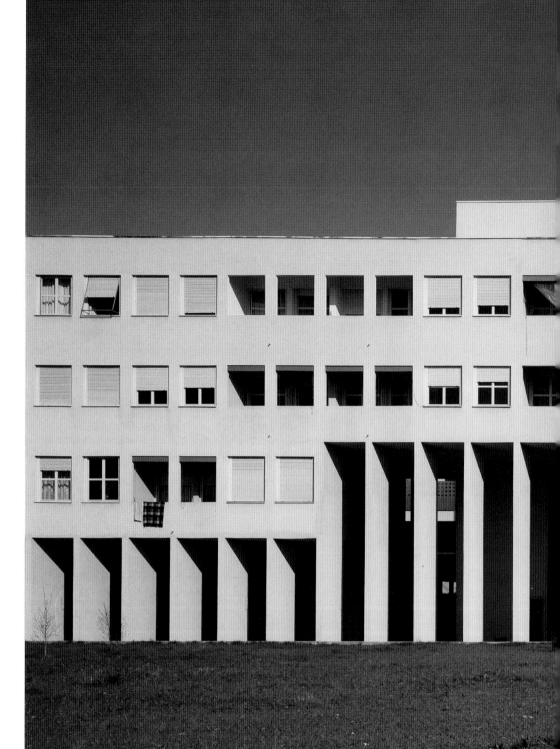

1 BEDROOM
2 LIVING/DINING ROOM
3 KITCHEN
4 BATHROOM
5 ENTRANCE

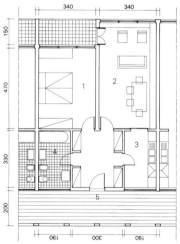

Typical unit plan of D block

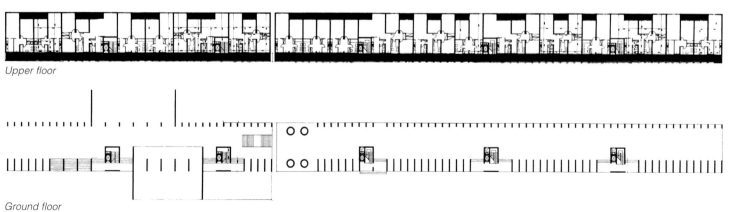

Upper floor

Ground floor

West facade of D block　D棟西面

East elevation

Portico of D block: view from south end　D棟の柱廊：南端より見る

Portico of D block: view from north　D棟の柱廊：北より見る

Portico of D block: view from south　D棟の柱廊：南より見る

1969–82
RALPH ERSKINE

BYKER REDEVELOPMENT
Newcastle upon Tyne, U.K.

View of north side of Wall Raby Gate section from east　レイビー・ゲイト部の〈壁〉北面を東より見る
View of Shipley Rise section of Wall from road on north　シップレイ・ライズ部の〈壁〉を北側道路より見る

West side of Gordon House at end of Byker Wall　バイカーの〈壁〉の西端部にあるゴードン・ハウス西面

Site plan

This submission relates to the sections of the Byker Redevelopment completed to date. The scheme is a comprehensive redevelopment of an inner city area of Newcastle, which seeks to re-house the existing community and retain its identity. Building work commenced in 1970.

The Site

The site is approximately 1 mile east of the centre of Newcastle. Further east are important sources of employment—shipbuilding and heavy engineering and to the north of the site is one of the principal shopping districts in Newcastle. The site is approximately 81 ha (200 acres) and is situated on a south-westerly slope. From the top of the hill to the lowest parts there is a difference of about 120 feet. The slope is steepest towards the top of the hill, with a gradient of up to 1 : 7. The site offers fine views across Newcastle and Gateshead with the Tyne Valley between.

Organization

The Perimeter Block had to be the first main stage of the project (after the small Pilot Scheme)—the only land available was where this building was to be constructed the Perimeter Block is now complete and the building makes a significant impact on both Byker and the city wide landscape. The character of the building has had design implications for the low-rise housing situated to the south. Although from the north side the length of the Perimeter Block is its most salient feature, when one passed through to the south side then sections of the Perimeter Block are experienced as integral parts of easily defined neighbourhoods consisting also of low-rise housing and link blocks. These 'link' blocks, filter down from the height of the adjacent section of Perimeter Block to that of the low-rise housing. In this pedestrian segregated redevelopment, the low-rise stages reflect lessons learned from the Pilot Scheme. This small project, which entailed collaboration and design participation with the tenants from layout plans to final completion, resulted in 46 dwellings being built on vacant land which was situated in the southern half of the redevelopment area; outside the area covered by the initial brief.

The success of the courtyard layout in the Pilot Scheme has resulted in further development. The courtyards have been protected from becoming principle pedestrian routes by being semi-private, for the immediate residents only, by the introduction of gates at the entry points. Each phase of the low-rise, whilst featuring the same overall design vocabulary has its own distinctive neighbourhood character which has been determined by both design and elevation variations. Some phases highlight the 'group of houses' character, whilst in others, these groups become obvious from within the courtyards, but appear as terraces from the main pedestrian and emergency access routes. In some phases there is a combination of the two ideas. In addition, variety on color schemes and the use of either timber or brick cladding gives specific identity to small groups of houses within a phase.

To take advantage of the view that the south westerly slope affords for low-rise housing as well as for the Perimeter Block, houses built along the contours rather than across them and the roof pitch is kept to a minimum—about 5 degrees being the norm. This layout also reduces the adverse effects of the hill for residents, who hitherto have had to cope with an up to 1 : 7 hill.

Within each phase are other community facilities. Hobby rooms serving small groups of houses have been included which can be used by individual tenants or resident's groups. Other community buildings already existed, and are renovated or replaced with new buildings. There are one or two new corner shops in each phase. Schools, churches and pubs are being retained or replaced, but the overall provision is the same as in old Byker. Many of these existing facilities are situated either in the middle or towards the top of the redevelopment area.

View of north side of Byker Wall from west (Raby Gate section)
バイカーの〈壁〉北面を西より見る（レイビー・ゲイト部）

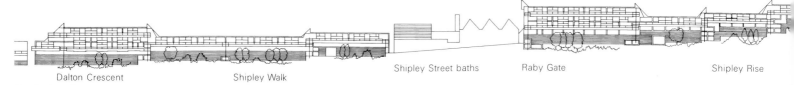

Dalton Crescent　　　Shipley Walk　　　Shipley Street baths　　Raby Gate　　　Shipley Rise

South elevation

North side of Wall at Shipley Walk: entrance gate through building
シップレイ・ウォークの〈壁〉北面：バイカー内への門が建物を貫通している

この計画は，ニューカッスル市内のバイカー地区について，既存の劣悪な居住環境を再開発し，同時にその独自のコミュニティを存続させる目的で，1970年に開始された。

敷地
ニューカッスル市の中心から東へ1マイルの地域で，さらにその東には造船所と重工業の工場地帯がひろがり，北側には，ニューカッスルでも有数のショッピング地域が控えている。敷地は81ヘクタール（200エーカー）の広さを持つ南西向きの斜面で，丘の頂上と麓の高低差は120フィート，最大勾配は7分の1に達する。丘の上からは，ニューカッスル市全域はもちろん，タイン河対岸のゲーツ・ヘッドまでが一望できる。

全体計画
まず，ペリメーター・ブロックの建設が，第1段階として遂行されることになった。ペリメーター・ブロックの完成によって，バイカー地区の景観は一変した。北側からみると，その巨大な壁面が延々とつづく印象を受けるが，南側を歩いている時は，ブロックの各部分が，低層住宅や中層のリンク・ブロックと結びついて小さな近隣集合をつくり，それらの連続として感じられる。リンク・ブロックは，ペリメーター・ブロックと低層住宅との高低差を連続的につなぐ働きをする。低層住宅の計画は，パイロット計画から学んだ様々な教訓を受けて行われた。パイロット計画は，最初のレイアウトから最終的な入居に至るまで，入居予定者との徹底的な話し合いと設計への参加を通して実行された。対象地域は，南半分の敷地内にある空地で，全体で46戸が計画された。パイロット計画において，中庭が好評を博したので，続く計画では，さらにこれが展開された。中庭は，セミ・プライベートな空間として，通行路にならないように保護策を構じ，住戸への導入部として，住戸専有の空間とした。

低層住宅は，各グループが集合としてのアイデンティティを持つように，集合の形態やエレベーションなどに様々なデザイン上の配慮を行った。集合の形は，中庭からみた形である場合や歩行者道からみたテラスの表情である場合など様々である。

南西向きの斜面による景観を活かすために，住戸はできるだけ等高線に沿って配置し，屋根勾配も，最低5度を規準とした。こうした配慮によって，最大7分の1という勾配の傾斜面に対する住民の抵抗感を軽減できたようだ。

各住区には共用施設も建設されている。小グループ毎に趣味の部屋があり，賃貸してもグループで使用しても良い。各住区には1, 2個所にコーナー・ショップがある。学校，教会，パブは既存のものをそのまま使うか，移設するかしている。これらは大体丘の中腹か，幾分頂上寄りに配置された。

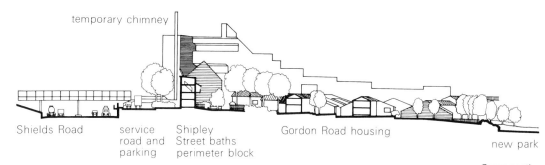

Cross section

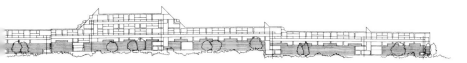

South side of Raby Gate: small garden and plaza surrounded by crescent building　レイビー・ゲイト南面：小さな庭と広場が湾曲した建物に囲まれている

Access deck and balconies in alternate position (Dalton Crescent)　交互に配されたアクセス・デッキとバルコニー（ドルトン・クレッセント）

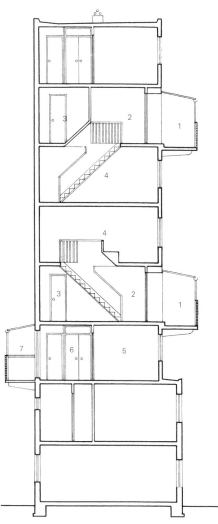

Section (wall-building, maisonette type)

1 ENTRANCE
2 DINING ROOM
3 KITCHEN
4 LIVING ROOM
5 BEDROOM
6 BATHROOM
7 BALCONY

View of Shipley Walk and Raby Gate from Dalton Crescent
ドルトン・クレッセントよりシップレイ・ウォークとレイビー・ゲイトを望む

View of access deck アクセス・デッキを見る

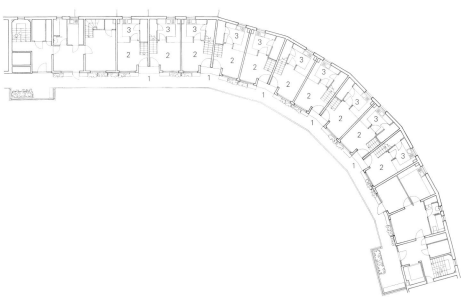

Level 4 (partial plan)

57

West side of Tom Collins House at Dunn Terrace　ダン・テラスのトム・コリンズ・ハウス西面

View of Dunn Terrace from balcony on west side of Gordon House　ゴードン・ハウスの西側バルコニーよりダン・テラスを見る

Site plan (Dunn Terrace)

South side of Dunn Terrace　ダン・テラス南面

Ground floor and landscape (Tom Collins House) S=1:700

1. ACCESS DECK
2. DINING ROOM
3. KITCHEN
4. LIVING ROOM
5. BEDROOM
6. BATHROOM
7. STORAGE
8. BALCONY
9. TERRACE
10. LOBBY
11. WARDEN
12. LAUNDRY
13. TV ROOM
14. SERVERY
15. RESIDENTS LOUNGE
16. CONSERVATORY
17. PARKING

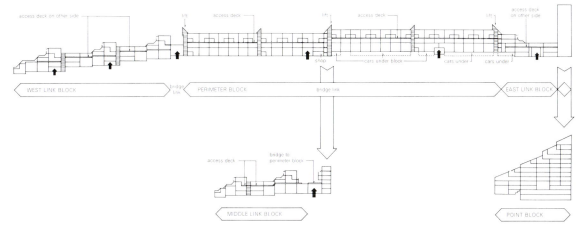

Section S=1:700

1970–72
KISHO KUROKAWA

NAKAGIN CAPSULE TOWER
Tokyo, Japan

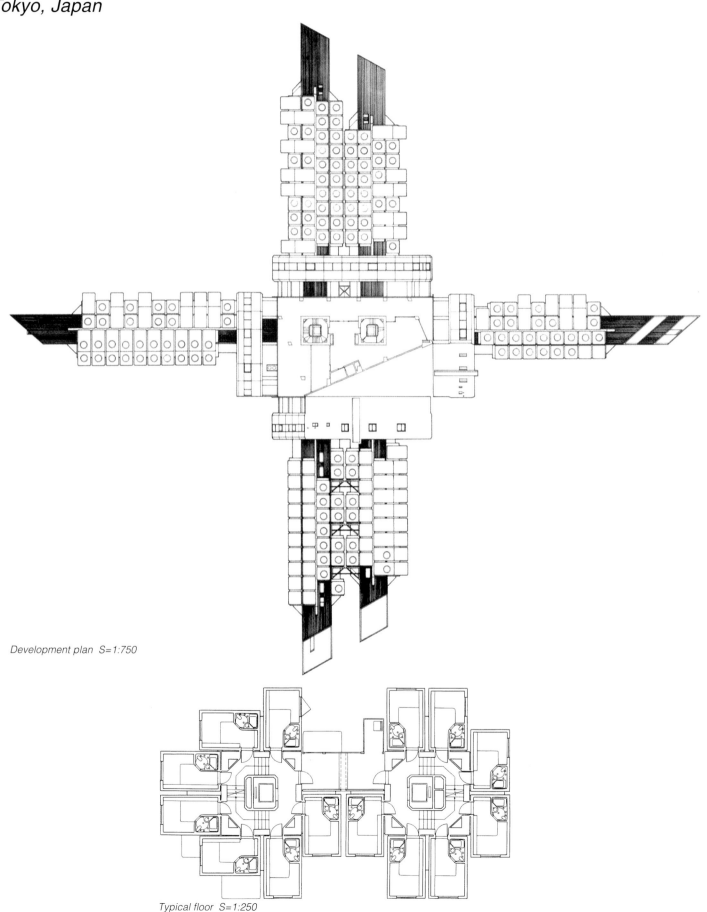

Development plan S=1:750

Typical floor S=1:250

Overall view from south　南側全景

Upward view from southwest 南西面見上げ

The Nakagin Capsule Tower is the world's first capsule architecture built for actual use. Capsule architecture design, establishment of the capsule as room and insertion of the capsule into a mega-structure, expresses its contemporaneousness with other works of liberated architecture from the later 1960's, in particular England's Archigram Group, France's Paul Memon, and Yona Friedman

The Nakagin Capsule Tower takes on the challenge of the issue of whether mass production can express a diverse new quality. The Tower also strives to establish a space for the individual as a criticism to the Japan that modernized without undergoing any establishment of an "self".

Kurokawa developed the technology to install the capsule units into a concrete core with only 4 high-tension bolts, as well as making the units detachable and replaceable. The capsule is designed to accommodate the individual as either an apartment or studio space, and by connecting units can also accommodate a family. Complete with appliances and furniture, from audio system to telephone, the capsule interior is pre-assembled in a factory off-site. The interior is then hoisted by crane and fastened to the concrete core shaft.

The Nakagin Capsule Tower realizes the ideas of metabolism, exchangeability, recycleablity as the prototype of sustainable architecture.

Kisho Kurokawa

Interior: bathroom on left and den on right 内観：左は浴室，右は書斎

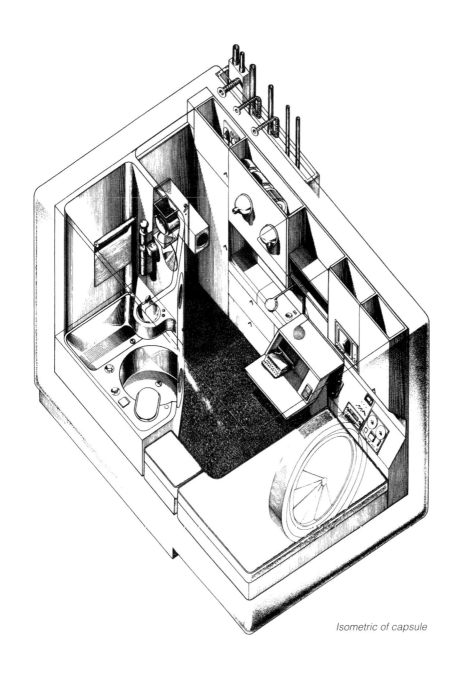

Isometric of capsule

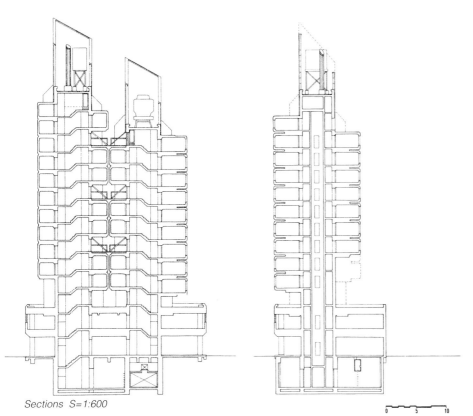

Sections S=1:600

世界で初めて実用化されたカプセル建築。1960年代前後に、イギリスのアーキグラム・グループや、フランスのポール・メモン、ヨナ・フリードマン等、建築を脱構築して、その部屋をカプセルとして自立させたり、メガストラクチャーにカプセル建築をとりつける構想と同時代性をもっている。

ここでは、プレハブ（量産）でありながら多様性という新しい質を表現できるかどうかという新しい課題の対する挑戦と、自我の自立という個人主義を経ることなく近代化してしまった日本への批判として、自立する個の空間を目指している。

技術的には4本の高張力ボルトのみでコンクリートコアシャフトに取付けられたカプセルは、実際に取りはずして新しいカプセルと交換されるよう、技術開発がなされている。カプセル建築は、単身者用の宿泊、デン（書斎）として想定されたが、家族用としては、数個を扉でつなぐことによって可能となるよう計画された。カプセルの内装は、電化製品や家具、オーディオ、ＴＶ、電話まで工場でセットされ、現地でクレーン車によって吊上げれらてシャフトに固定された。

新陳代謝、取換え、リサイクルを実現したサスティナブル建築の原型でもある。

（黒川紀章）

Redevelopment of the ruin of cement factory　セメント工場跡地の再開発計画

Walden 7 creates a space that permits itself to be distinguished from it's mediocre surroundings and which at the same time stimulates an animation and internal community life. Consequently there is a distinctive treatment of facades and spaces. In the first phase, already built, the exterior facade gives the impression of a wall that represents an alternative to suburban architecture.

It has the image of a solemn and monumental fortress entirely covered with tiles which opens itself to the exterior by great vertical openings that seem like immense windows, several floors high. This gives austerity to the monument, and at the same time, in spite of its solidity appears penetrated by the wind and open space.

The space stays differentiated and isolated from the exterior in order to be better used by the people. This is a recuperation of the street and the square for the benefit of the community. It attempts to generate an interior world distinct from the external chaos.

The order of the interiors of the apartments consists of the definition of various functional elements leaving the rest of the space usable as living area. This is a way to break from the tradition of completely compartmentalized spaces, so that the definition of what is communal and private is left more open.

ウォールデン7はその周辺の平凡な環境のなかにあってひときわ目立つ空間をつくりあげるものであり，そこに生気を吹込むとともに内部のコミュニティの生活に刺激を与えることが目論まれている。それゆえそのファサードと空間の扱いにはかなり思いきった処理がなされている。すでに建設が終わった第1期工事においては，1個の壁体の如きイメージのファサードがつくられ，都市郊外の建築の採るべき道を示している。

この建物には堂々とした構えの城砦の如き趣きがあり，その表面は全面タイルでおおわれ，数階分の高さのある巨大な窓の如き細長い開口でのみ外部に接している。それはこの建物に，ある厳しさをそなえるとともに，また一方，この堅固な塊のなかを風が吹抜け，オープン・スペースが貫通するための手だてとなっている。

建物の内側の空間は人々にとって使いやすいよう，外部からはっきりと分け取られ独立させられている。これは道や広場をもう一度コミュニティ自身のためのものとして再生させる試みである。ここでは外部の喧騒からまったく隔絶した内部世界を構築することが求められているのである。

Wall detail　壁面ディテール

Wall detail 壁面ディテール

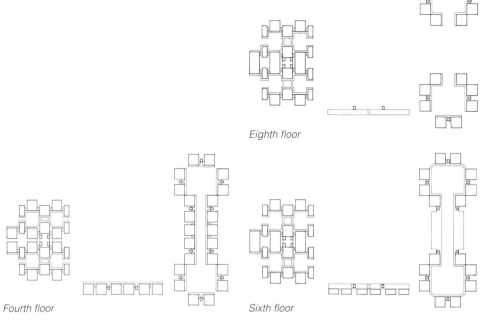

Eighth floor

Fourth floor   *Sixth floor*

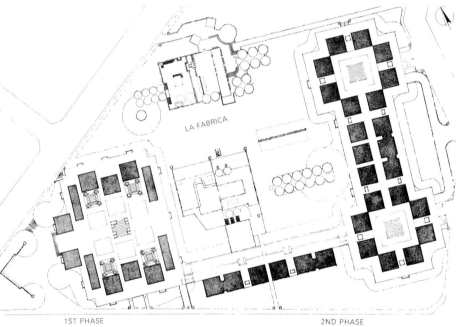

Site plan

Downward view of terraces テラスを見下ろす

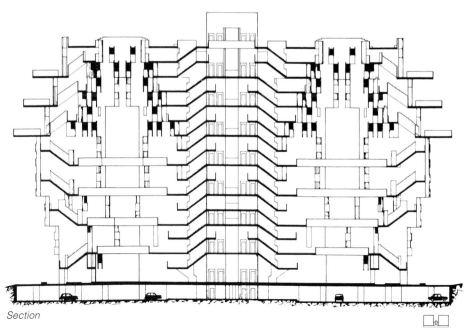

Section

Upward view from entrance hall　エントランス・ホール見上げ

Downward view of pathway　通路を見下ろす

Pathway on upper floor　上階通路

Entrance hall: view toward entrance エントランス・ホール：入口を見る

Pathway facing patio パティオに面した通路

Downward view of patio with fountain 噴水のあるパティオを見下ろす

Upper part of patio: view toward outside パティオ上部：外を見る

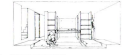
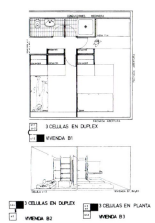

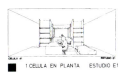

Unit plans

Swimming pool on roof terrace ルーフテラスのスイミング・プール

Roof terrace ルーフテラス

◁▽ *Interior of unit* 住戸内部

1970-76
LUCIEN KROLL

QUARTIER DES FACULTES MEDICALES
Brussels, Belgium

View from west. From left to right: Restaurant, Mémé, Fachiste, Ecole 西より見る。左から右：レストラン，メメ，ファシスト，エコールの各棟

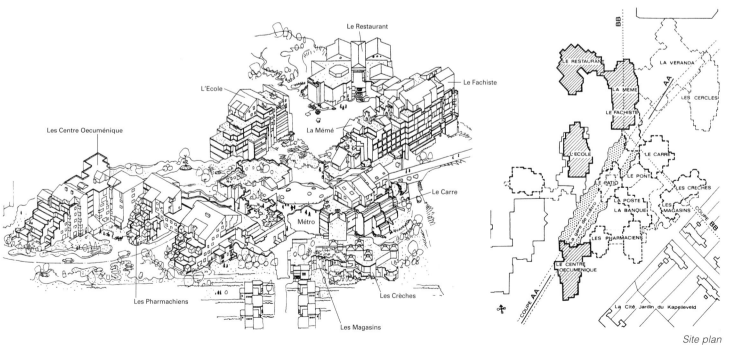

Site plan

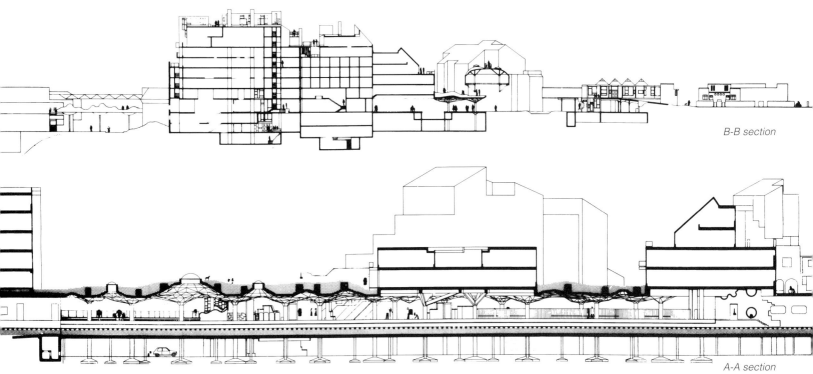

B-B section

A-A section

Mémé (left) and Fachiste (right)　メメ（左），ファシスト（右）

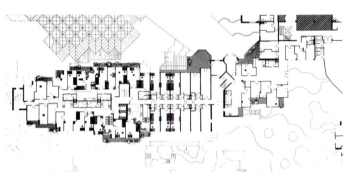

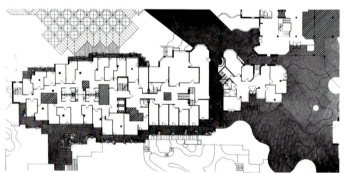

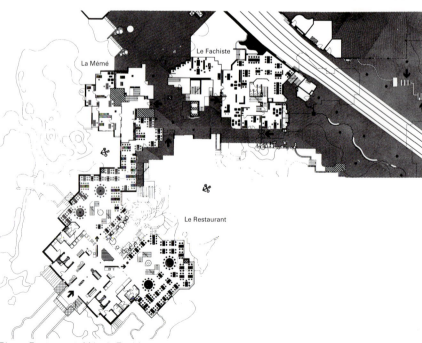

Plans: Restaurant, Mémé, Fachiste

Restaurant (left), Mémé (center, left) and Fachiste (center, right)　レストラン（左），メメ（正面左），ファシスト（正面右）

Access to Restaurant　レストラン入口

View from northeast toward Mémé (right) and Fachiste (left)　北東よりメメ（右），ファシスト（左）を見る

The entire program consists of 20 apartments, 60 one-room flats, 200 bachelor rooms, 200 rooms grouped in apartments, 6 communal houses with 18 rooms each and the premises of the Mémé.

In addition, restaurant seating for 750, cultural and religious centres, a cinema, a theatre and workshop; a nursery, a kindergarten, the students' welfare service, administration and general services.

Finally, of importance to the whole district and covering 3,500 m², a post office, services, shops and small typical restaurants and this program has covered 40,000 m².

Round about 1968, the Catholic University was preparing to leave the old town of Louvain and build a big hospital in Brussels together with medical faculties and all the residential installations necessary for day and night. The authorities had drawn up an extremely 19th century master plan (rigid zoning and glory of the institution). Sincerely open (for the time) to a certain amount of consultation, it proposed this plan to the medical students: they refused it as they did not want to be formed by this type of urbanism and become typical overspecialized, privileged, non-social, comfortable doctors. They wanted this centralized image of the institution broken up and mixed with other residents and the neighbouring districts, and to accept the residents' initiatives in a certain form of joint management. The authorities refused (technical requirements, etc.), but at least the students were able to propose their own architect. That was when they discovered and adopted us: since then relations between the two sides have no longer respected the usual hierarchy.

In this miraculous situation we cooperated with very active students and representatives of the institution who were lucid, competent and extremely receptive. (It was only later that they degenerated and became bureaucratic). It was at that very moment that the choice was being made: on the one side the superficial, paternal order, and its artificial image. We actually went in the other direction: the organic, the diverse, everyday culture decolonization, the subjective, an image compatible with self-administrative attitudes, in short an urban texture with its contradictions, its element of chance and its convergences. A political rather than an aesthetic project.

A great many meetings with the future residents, the authorities and tradesmen: many elements must be present if a variegated setting is to be created. This policy must be apparent through the architectural arguments wherever we were able to invent them or deviate them.

The general outline of the university site is an attempt to continue the existing district, sometimes going as far as mimicry: there is no sharply-defined border. The site includes elements appropriate to the district such as metro station, a post office, business premises, etc...

No large, regular blocks, but irregular, random shapes, communicating on various levels, entrances and exits everywhere, as much vegetation as possible on the buildings, all the "ordinary" materials and elements in use at present in the forms and dimensions and random colors as in a setting constructed and transformed over a period of years. All functions are mixed together: the rector works above the primary school children, and underneath the young couples' accommodation.

The housing is extremely varied. The first group of student rooms in the Mémé (the "maison médicale") have partitions which the students themselves decide. Others in the attics were entirely designed by groups of students. In order to be certain of avoiding the conditioning of a regular structure pillars were placed in irregular "walks" made possible by the "floor-plate-mushroom" system after painful struggles with the "rationalists".

In accordance with the same policy we decided on open prefabrication: all spaces are governed by a system of modular co-ordination inspired by the SAR in Eindhoven.

△▷ *Loft at Mémé: handmade fixture/partition by students*
メメ内のロフト。パーティション，建具は学生たちの手づくりによる

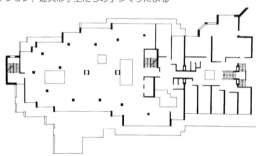

Plan: Mémé (floor-plate-mushroom strucural system made to avoid the regular structural pillars)

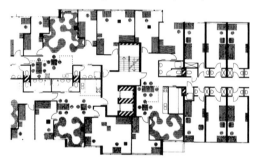
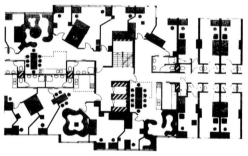

△▽ *Mémé: layout variation by students*

Ecole (left), Mémé and Fachiste (right)　エコール（左）とメメ，ファシスト（右）

　全体計画には20戸の一般住戸，60戸のワンルームタイプの住戸，200室の単身者用住戸，アパートの形にまとめられた200室分の個室，それぞれ18室からなる六つの共同住宅，それに〈メメ〉の施設が含まれている。

　その他，750席のレストラン，文教センターと教会，映画館，劇場，工房，保育園，幼稚園，学生のための福祉サービス施設，および一般管理施設がある。

　最後に，総計3,500平米あまりの重要な地域施設として，郵便局，サービス施設，店舗，専門レストランが計画され，計画全体は40,000平米にも及ぶ。

　1968年頃のことである。カトリック大学は古都ルーヴェンからブリュッセルに移転し，そこに医学部の諸施設と共に大きな病院を建設し，あわせて宿舎をはじめとする生活施設をつくる準備を進めていた。そのときすでに大学当局は，固定的にゾーニングされた栄光ある学園といった感じの，きわめつきの19世紀的なマスタープランを持っていた。その当時としては民主的な措置であったと評価できるのだが，当局はある程度この案について協議したいということで，マスタープランを医学部の学生に提示したわけである。学生たちは，この種のアーバニズムに従って体制化され，専門馬鹿の特権階級，非社会的で安穏とした医者の典型とされるのは御免とばかりに，この案を蹴った。彼らは，このように中央集権的な学園像を打破し他の住民や近隣地域と混然一体となり，何らかの形の共同運営方式により居住者側でイニシアティヴを発揮したいと考えていた。技術的な問題やそ

の他の理由によって，当局側はこれを拒否した。しかし，学生は彼らの側で建築家を指名できるという権利を最低限留保することができた。われわれが彼らの目にとまり採用されたのは，このときのことである。以来，両者の間では通常のヒエラルキーは，もはや存在しないと了解されている。

　このような奇跡的な状況の下で，われわれは活動的な学生や学校側の代表者と共に作業を進めた。彼らは明晰かつ有能で，きわめて理解力に富んでいた。彼らの姿勢が退歩し官僚的になっていったのは後になってからのことである。しかしそのときこそまさに選択がなされようとしていたときでもあった。一応それは，外面的には父性的な秩序を持ち，それだけにわざとらしいイメージのものであった。われわれは実際には反対の行き方をとった。有機的な質，多様性，日常的な文化の解放，主観性，自立的な姿勢にふさわしいイメージ，つまり手短かに言えば，矛盾や偶然性，多くの収束点を併せ持ったひとつの都市的なテクスチャーということである。美を追求するというよりは政治的なプロジェクトであった。

　敷地の大まかな輪郭は，既存の街なみをそのまま引き延ばそうということで，時として〈擬態〉と言う方が当っているかも知れないほどである。その中には，地下鉄の駅や郵便局，商業建築など，地域施設としてふさわしいと思われるものが含まれている。

　大きな規則的な形の街区はとらず，そのかわりに，不規則なとりどりの形，いろいろなレベルでの往来，そこかしこの出入口，できるだけ多くの植栽，今日よく見かける〈ありふれた〉大きさと

形を持った素材やエレメント，何年もの間にわたってつくられ，つくり直されてきた環境に見られるようなとりどりの配色といったものが求められている。例えば，小学校の児童の頭上，若夫婦の住居の足下で牧師が礼拝をとり行なうというように，すべての機能がごちゃ混ぜにされている。

　住居計画はきわめて多様である。〈メメ〉（メゾン・メディカル）の最初のグループは，学生自身が間仕切の配置を決めている。この他，ロフトはグループを組んだ学生によって設計されたものである。規則的な位置にある構造体の制約を避けるため，〈合理主義者〉たちとの厄介な議論のあげく無梁版構造によって，柱を不規則に配置する方法をとることができた。

　同じポリシーに従って，われわれはオープンシステムによるプレファブリケーションを採用することにした。すべての空間には，アイントホーフェンでのSARの試みを踏襲して，同じモジュラー・コーディネーションのシステムが適用されている。

Centre Oecuménique　サントル・エキュメニク

△▷ *Centre Oecuménique: staircase*　サントル・エキュメニク：階段室

Centre Oecuménique: staircase section

Ecole エコール

1977–81
MANTEOLA, SÁNCHEZ GOMEZ, SANTOS, SOLSONA, VIÑOLY

MANANTIALES HOUSING
Punta del Este, Uruguay

Central plaza 中央広場

East elevation 東面

Situation:
This housing complex, of 100 units, with the distinctive characteristics of a holiday seaside village, has been erected in an area on the Atlantic coast not far from Punta del Este, a seaside resort in the Republic of Uruguay.

Design:
The complex respects and adheres to the conditions of the area. Its layout rests on two circulation routes external to the site; it preserves and reinforces the natural slope down to the beach in a compact construction, closed to the street and open to the sea. This mass is cut through by vaulted pedestrian streets which give access to the housing units and lead to the central green area and the seaside; it is also cut across by a longitudinal pedestrian street, shaping closed small squares, protected from the wind, where different shops have been located. A large plaza, sculptured on the floor collects the different walks and opens out to the green area by the beach and

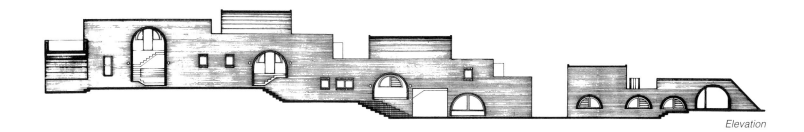
Elevation

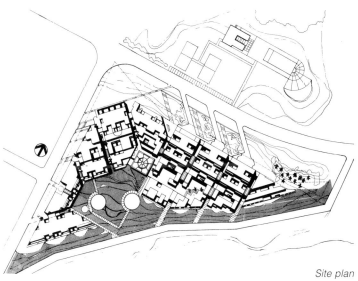
Site plan

the sea.

The diversity of housing typology, the variety of solutions given to the units, the terraces with pergolas and trillages which sunshade them, the vaults over the transverse streets defining the access to the dwellings, all these elements create a varied, diversified scenery under a strong sunshine. The sea, which all the houses view, is a constant point of reference.

This variety of situations is rationalized in a concrete structural grid of 3.70 m x 3.70 m which orders the apparent labyrinth of the design.

Materials:

Only one material: brick; shapes the whole complex. Walls, floors, vaults, terraces have been built of this material which in some cases, has been painted in different hues of red without covering its texture.

Natural wood is used for pergolas, trillages and verandahs, and white marble gives shape to the square.

Apartment blocks with open plaza and pedestrian street　広場とアーケードを持つ住棟部分

Pedestrian street with brick arch and vaulted roofs　レンガのアーチとヴォールト屋根で構成された通路

Partly covered street　所々覆われた通路

Apartment entry　住戸入口

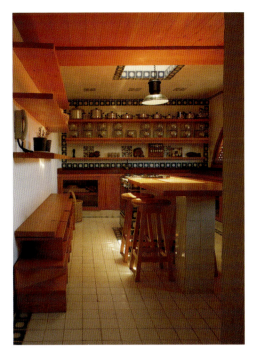

◁△▽ *Interior of apartment* 住戸内部

敷地：
この集合住宅は100戸の住戸をもち，海岸沿いの休暇村の特徴を備えている。それは，ウルグアイのシーサイド・リゾート，プンタ・デル・エステからさほど遠くない大西洋岸地方に建てられた。

デザイン：
この集合住宅は，この地方の諸状況を尊重しあくまでそれに固執している。レイアウトは敷地の外を巡る2本のサーキュレーション・ルートに基づいている。街路に対して閉じ，海に対して開いたコンパクトな建物群は，海に向かう自然のスロープを抱き強調する形をとる。建物群にはヴォールトのかかった歩道が通される。その歩道は住戸へのアクセスとなり，また中央の緑地や海岸にも続いている。さらに，縦方向の歩道も通されるが，それは風から守られた小さな広場を形成し，そこにはいろいろな店舗が設けられる。大きな広場はさまざまな歩道が集まる所につくられ，海岸のそばの緑地に向かって開いている。

多様な住戸タイプ，住戸に与えられたさまざまな解答，住戸に影をつけるパーゴラや格子のついたテラス，住戸へのアクセスとなる横方向の街路上に架かるヴォールト，これらすべての要素が強い日差しの下で多様な変化に富む景観をつくり出す。全住戸がのぞんでいる海は，住居群の焦点である。3.70メートル角のコンクート構造グリッドがさまざまな問題を合理化し，迷路のような外観に秩序を与えている。

材料：
煉瓦という単一の材料が全体をかたちづくっている。壁，床，ヴォールト，テラスはこの材料でつくられているが，場合によってはテクスチャーを変えることなく違った赤色ペイントが塗られている。パーゴラ，格子，ベランダには木が使われ，白い大理石が広場をかたちづくっている。

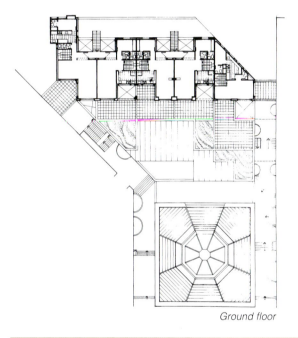
Ground floor

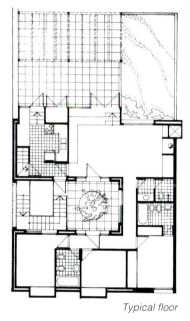
Typical floor

81

1978-82
ARQUITECTONICA

THE ATLANTIS
Miami, Florida, U.S.A.

Overall view from northeast　北東側全景

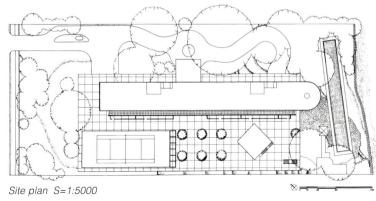

Site plan　S=1:5000

Aerial view from west 西側全景

The Atlantis is a 96-unit 20-story condominium apartment building at the edge of Biscayne Bay on the former estate of Mary Tiffany Bingham, sister of Louis C. Tiffany and wife of Hiram Bingham who discovered Machu Picchu. Her mansion has been renovated and restored to become a club house for the condominium.

The lot was divided into 2 zones: a romantic garden on the north, which is the entrance, and a utilitarian podium on the south side which hides the required parking and has tennis courts and a small health club on its surface. The pure zoning-generated prism was transformed from a rectangular solid by curving the eastern end of the building and removing a 50 x 50 x 50 cube from the body of the prism. This cube becomes the health club on the podium and its void allows 8 apartments to share a sky patio with a free form jacuzzi and a palm tree. Additions to the pure volume are the four yellow triangular balconies oriented towards the best view on the north side and the red triangular prism on top which hides the cooling equipment. The building was conceived as a pure glass volume, however, its south face is masked by an oversized blue frame which corrects irregularities created by the cantilevered balconies and doubles as a brise-soleil.

View of rounded east end 曲面で構成される東端部

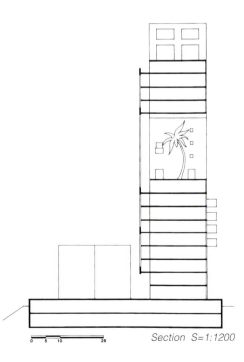

Section S=1:1200

ザ・アトランティスはビスケイン湾岸に建つ96戸／20階建のコンドミニアムである。ここは以前，ルイ・C・ティファニーの姉で，マチュ＝ピチュを発見したハイラム・ビンガムの妻，マリー・ティファニー・ビンガムの所有地であった。彼女の邸宅は改修・保存されてコンドミニアムのクラブハウスへと生まれ変わった。

　敷地は二つにゾーン分けされた。まず，入口となる北側のロマンティックな庭園部。そして南側の実用に即した基壇で，これは駐車場を下に隠し上部にテニスコートと小さなヘルスクラブを備える。二つのゾーンを分けるピュアな直方体は次のように変形される。東端にアールがつけられ，本体から50フィート角の立方体が切り取られた。この立方体が基壇上においてヘルスクラブとなり，くり貫かれた間隙は不定形のジャクジーと棕櫚(シュロ)の木を備えたスカイ・パティオとなり8戸のアパートに供される。また黄色い三角形のバルコニーが4段，北側の素晴らしい眺めに向けて，元の躯体に取り付き，頂部にはクーリング設備を隠す赤い三角錐が乗せられた。この建物は純粋なガラス箱として考えられていたのだが，オーバー・スケールの青いフレームが南面を覆い，それがキャンティレバーで突き出たバルコニーによって生じた不規則性を修正すると共にブリーズ・ソレイユとしての機能を果す。

View toward entrance エントランスを見る

Entrance エントランス

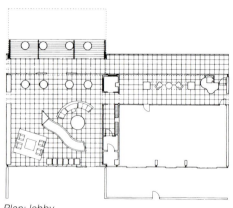

Plan: lobby

Sky patio with jacuzzi ジャグジーのあるスカイ・パティオ

Terrace on east 東側テラス

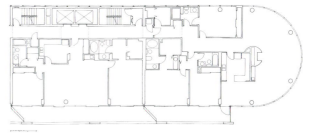
Typical floor

◁△ *Lobby* ロビー

1978–84
PIET BLOM

ARBRES/FORÊT D'HABITATIONS
Helmond, The Netherlands

Overall view of "trees of house" 〈住居の木〉全景

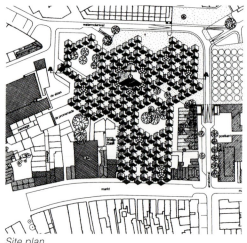

Site plan

Elevation: view from Ameidewal Street

Elevation: view from market side

Upward view of "trees of house": trunk of tree with reinforced concrete and residential part with wood 〈住居の木〉見上げ:幹はコンクリート造,住居部分は木造

Living room 居間

Dining room 食堂

<A place for an encounter> is the theme of this project. Located in a market, the site was used to be a Catholic convent. Many small retail stores line up on the ground level. A promonade, parking and a library are also being planned. On top of these facilities, a group of houses is to be placed. This tactic should fill the new apartment complex with vigor during the day and also erase loneliness at night.

A hall for concerts, congregations and shows occupies the central area. The hall is surrounded by <special trees>, which are equipped with social functions. It can be said that the <special trees> are then surrounded by <trees of houses>.

The group of houses was initially planned for 200 units, but now 60 units are planned to be built. 3 units introduced in this article were built as an outset and the rest of 57 units will be built, seeing how the first 3 units go. The trunk of the <tree>, standing on a hexagonal grid, is made of reinforced concrete. The houses are structured with wood and quite a few openings are made of glass. It is devised to catch light from the sky as well as from the street. Because the upper residential area is made compact and is connected to each other, a person does not need to go down outside to visit the adjacent unit.

<Trees> gather and make a forest. People shall enjoy everyday lives in this forest.

〈出会いの場〉がこの計画のテーマである。敷地は市場のなか，カソリック尼僧院の跡地である。地上には小さな店舗が数多く設けられ，プロムナード，パーキング，図書館なども計画されている。その上に住居群がのせられるわけである。こうすれば，この新開の団地の昼は活気に満ち，夜も淋しくはならないだろう。

センターの部分には，コンサート，会合，ショーなどのためのホールがある。このホールは社会的な機能をそなえた〈特別の木〉に囲まれている。その〈特別の木〉の周りを，さらに〈住居の木〉がとり巻いているわけである。

この住居群は，最初200戸が計画されたが現段階では60戸が実施予定である。その手はじめにここに紹介する3戸が建てられ，様子を見て残りの57戸がつくられることになっている。六角形グリッドの上に載ったこの〈木〉の幹にあたる部分はコンクリート造，住居部分は木造，ガラスの開口部も少なくない。空の光も地上の光もとり入れるようになっている。上部の住居部分はコンパクトであり，互いに連結されているから，隣に行くときには1度外に降りなくてもすむ。

〈木〉は集まって森になる。人々はこの森のなかで，日々の生活を楽しむことになるだろう。

Kitchen　台所

Details of windows　窓部分詳細

Staircase on fourth floor　4階にある階段

Family room on third floor　3階の家族室

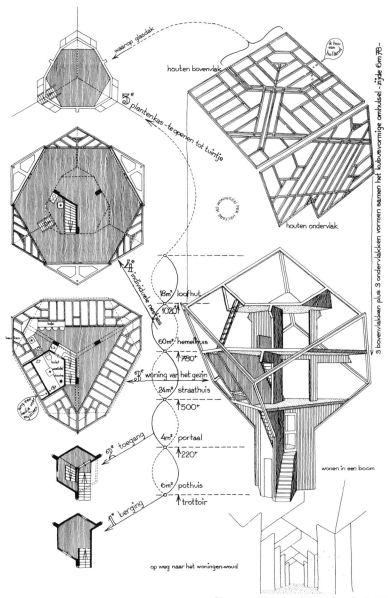
Plans and details of structure　S=1:150

1978–83
RICARDO BOFILL / TALLER DE ARQUITECTURA

LES ESPACES D'ABRAXAS
Marne-la-Vallée, France

Overall view

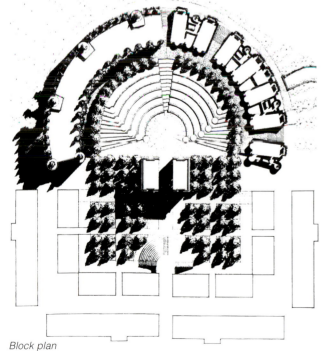
Block plan

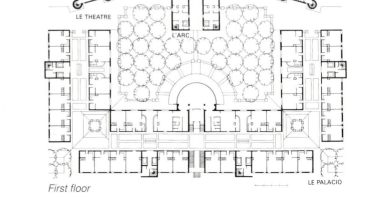
First floor

Le Théâtre: internal facade 〈劇場〉:内側外観

View toward Le Palais through main axis 主軸を通して〈宮殿〉を見る

Plaza between Le Théâtre (left) and L'Arc (right)　〈劇場〉(左)と〈凱旋門〉(右)の間の広場

L'Arc　〈凱旋門〉

Facade detail of Le Théâtre 〈劇場〉の外観詳細

Interior of Le Théâtre 〈劇場〉内部

Project

Le Palais, Le Théâtre and L'Arc are all created around the same 6.07-meter framework, while both the depth of the housing units and the width of the inner street are 8.10 meters.

Le Palais is a block of 400 units. Three vertical cores of communication links—lifts, staircases and technical (service) shafts—serve all units. All the external covered streets (galleries) are arranged to provide a system of access to each housing unit. Most of the units comprise two levels and face in two directions: one towards the outside and the other towards the internal road. The housing units (of between two and five rooms) are arranged in the following way: the hallway giving directly onto the dining room, kitchen, living room and an internal staircase; on the lower floor are the bedroom and bathroom. The structure is formed by the support walls and even if the shape forms an X, the weight is distributed vertically on the foundations which are built on piles. The building's wind bracing is ensured by the vertical communication cores which are rigid structures and by the floor itself.

The facade's reinforced concrete panels are fastened to the support walls and ensure the ultimate rigidity of the building. To avoid construction problems, the structures and the facades must be built simultaneously.

Le Théâtre is a more private building. The vertical communication links (lifts, staircases) serve, across entrance halls, two flats of two, three, four, or five rooms per floor, which means that there are 130 doubly oriented housing units facing the interior of Le Théâtre and the exterior.

The housing units are constructed in such a way that the kitchen, dining room and bathrooms are disposed around an axis perpendicular to the support walls. The attics overhang and their housing units have private, individual terraces which face the interior.

L'Arc is also made up of four parallel support walls. The central framework is hollow up to the sixth level and from there on, solid. The prefabricated panels are assembled from the sort of panels used in the two other buildings. There are two cores of vertical communication links in L'Arc (lifts, technical shafts), from which one enters an individual housing unit. The pillars of L'Arc are organized as duplexes.

The roofs of both L'Arc and Le Théâtre have been made into gardens which are overlooked by Le Palais.

A Series of Inversions

The deterioration of a town leads, eventually, to its disappearance suburbs and public housing evoke our urban cancer and are synonymous with a dull, if regular existence.

Marne-la-Vallée poses these very problems, but here a resolution has been effected in architectural terms, and this project is a program of public housing for workers. As a residential area, it privileges the break with the world of work, allowing a reevaluation of the milieu to which it belongs, and its inherent values. The composition as a whole forms a unity comprising three buildings and a fourth, equally vital element, open space.

The work fashions a closed universe which becomes a powerful communal structure; the open spaces create urban windows and doors which partially divide the town, when the latter is seen as a set. As in a painting, external reality is framed and this withdrawal, this distancing, questions its nature. These inversions are only really effective because the space is highly organized.

Overall view of Le Palais 〈宮殿〉全景

Facade detail of Le Palais 〈宮殿〉の外観詳細

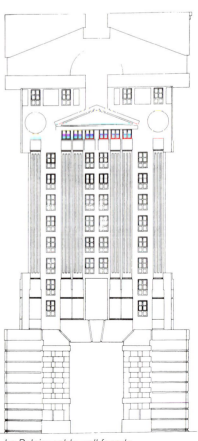
Le Palais: gable wall facade

◁△*Le Palais: interior street* 〈宮殿〉：内部の街路

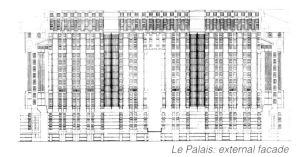

Le Palais: external facade　　　　　　　　　*Le Palais: internal facade*

一連の反転

都市の荒廃はその滅亡をもたらしかねない。郊外住宅地，低所得者用の公共集合住宅は，都市の癌を想起させ，希望のない日常生活と同義語と化している。

こうした状況の中でつくり出されたマルヌ＝ラ＝ヴァレ・ニュータウンは建築の回復をめざしたもので，ここで練られたのは労働者の住居となる社会的性格を持った集合住宅のプログラムである。住宅地ゆえに，労働の世界と切り離されるという特権を享受し，その置かれた環境ならびにその場所に内在する価値を生かした休息地を築くことが可能である。ここでの建築群は，三つの建造物からなる量体に加えて，同じく決定因子となる第4のエレメント，すなわち空隙をも示している。

建築は，コミュニティを強く構造づける一つの閉じた宇宙を生み出す。空隙は，都市の一部を切り取って都市を装飾として見せる都市の窓，都市の門を築き上げる。外界の現実にあたかも画布のごとく縁どりが施され，此方から彼方の隔たりを通して問が投げかけられる。こうした反転は，空間がほどよく組織化されて初めて実効を得る。

プロジェクト

〈宮殿〉，〈劇場〉，〈凱旋門〉はいずれも6.07メートルからなる同一のグリッド・システムによって構成されている。住戸の奥行は8.10メートル。屋内街路の幅も8.10メートルである。

〈宮殿〉は400戸を収めた集合住宅である。エレベータ，階段，パイプ・スペースを収めた垂直交通「コア」が3本設けられ，そこから各住戸に達することになる。外部に出た屋根付の通路（廊下）は全体でおのおのの住戸へのアクセス・システムをかたちづくる。住戸の大半は2層にわたったメゾネットとして構想され，外側および内側の通路両方向におのおの面している。2室から5室のタイプまで多様に配されたこれらの住戸は，以下のような平面配置となっている。玄関から各部屋へダイレクトに続く廊下を通って，食堂，台所，居間，室内階段，そして下層には寝室と浴室。建物は壁構造で支えられ，全体の形がX形となっていながらも，荷重は杭上の基礎まで鉛直に伝達される。水平力に対しては，剛構造たる垂直動線コア間に設けられた梁とブレース，ならびに床自体をもって支えることになる。

ファサード・パネルは鉄筋コンクリート製，構造壁に取り付けられ，建物の剛性を最終的に保証する。組み立て作業の困難を避けるため，構造体とファサードは同時に組み上げる。

〈劇場〉はより私的領域の高まった建物である。エレベータ，階段といったおのおのの垂直動線は，各階で共有の玄関ホールを介してそれぞれ2戸の住戸に結ばれる。住戸タイプは2室型から5室型まで分かれ，いずれも劇場内部および外部の2面に面し，全体で130戸を数える。この住戸の平面は，構造壁に直交する軸を中心とし，一方に台所，食堂，浴室がとられている。最上階は張り出しており，内外にプライベートなテラスを持っている。

〈凱旋門〉も同じく平行する4構造壁から構成されている。中央のグリッドは6階まで吹き抜け，その上に建物を載せている。プレハブ・パネルは，他の二つの建物で用いられたパネルを混ぜ合わせたものである。この〈凱旋門〉には2本の垂直動線コア（エレベータ，パイプ・スペース）が設けられ，そこから各住戸へのアクセスがなされる。各々の柱はメゾネットに合わせて2層を突き抜けている。

〈劇場〉および〈凱旋門〉の屋根上には庭園がつくられ，〈宮殿〉からその様子が眺められる。

1978–99
TADAO ANDO

ROKKO HOUSING I, II, III
Kobe, Hyogo, Japan

Aerial view. From left to right (bottom to top): Rokko Housing I, II, III 空撮。左から右（下から上）：六甲の集合住宅 I, II, III

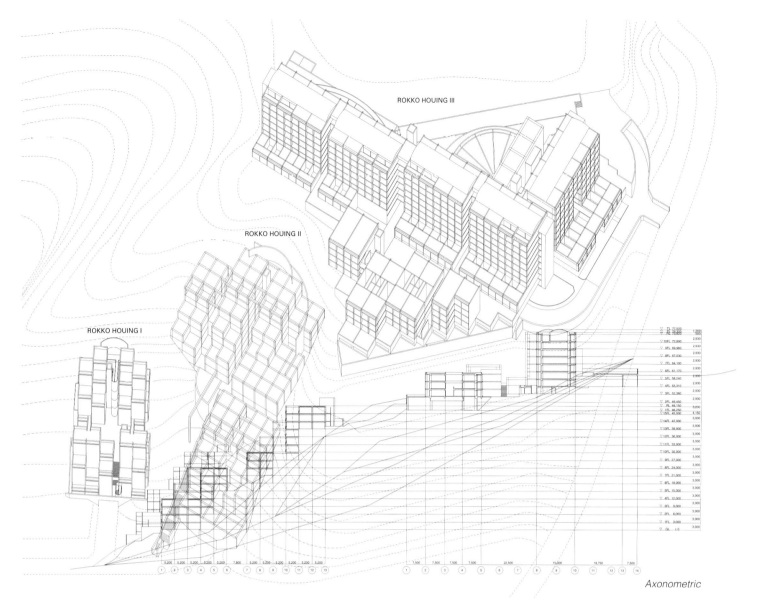

Axonometric

The site is situated on the hillside of Mount Rokko between Osaka and Kobe. Here, I have been involved in a project to build an apartment complex over three stages, starting in 1978.

Throughout the project, the underlying theme was to achieve a comfortable living space within a harsh natural environment, and to take advantage of the richness that is unique to this local setting. To take advantage of the distinct topography, I introduced a geometric structure with uniform framing into the vast unevenness of nature. This contrast generated numerous gaps and crevices, which helped me to create a variety of layouts, and inspire character into the land.

With the expansion of the complex, I became increasingly aware of the need for a public space. In addition to improving the stairs and terraces, an indoor athletic space was incorporated into the project during the second stage.

As the second stage came to a completion, I had already proposed the plans for the third stage that would be constructed on the adjacent land. With the effects of the Great Hanshin earthquake in 1995, however, the project also took on a meaning of restoration. In 2009, a medical complex that includes a general hospital and geriatrics services was completed just 200 meters west of the three apartments.

My hope is that passage of time will organically and boldly integrate the residential units and buildings with each other, nurturing a community that is centered around contemporary architecture.
Tadao Ando

敷地は，阪神間にある六甲の斜面地に位置する。そこで，1978年から，3期にわたって集合住宅の計画に関わってきた。

全期に一貫する主題は，厳しい条件の敷地に，いかにして生活空間を獲得し，そこにしかない豊かさを実現するか。特色ある地形を活かす手段として，不規則な自然の地形にあえて等質なフレームを持ち込む幾何学的構成を採用した。そこに生じるグリッドのズレと隙間に，各戸の間取りの多様さ，土地の個性を生み出す手掛かりを求めた。

規模の拡大につれて，より強く意識したのは，パブリックスペースの獲得である。特に2期では，階段，テラスの充実と共に，屋内アスレチック・スペースがプログラムに盛り込まれた。

2期の完成時点で，さらにその隣に3期計画を自主提案としてまとめていたが，その構想は1995年の阪神淡路大震災を経て，復興住宅の意味合いをもって実現されることになった。さらに2009年には，同じ斜面地にある，三つの集合住宅から西に200メートル離れた場所で，総合病院と老人医療の複合施設が完成している。

時間の経過が住戸と住戸，住棟と住棟を有機的かつダイナミックに結びつけ，現代建築による集落の風景が育まれていくことを期待している。

（安藤忠雄）

Rokko Housing I, 1978-83

△▷ *Courtyard* 中庭

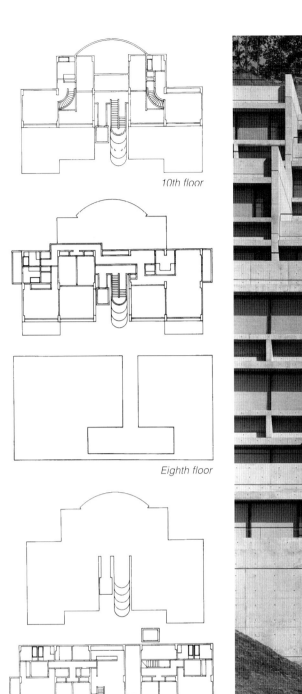

10th floor

Eighth floor

Second floor S=1:500

Front elevation アプローチ側壁面

◁△ Interior of apartment 住戸内部

Phase I (left) and II (right)   I期（左）とII期（右）

Rokko Housing II, 1985-93

Plaza on middle level   中間階の屋外プラザ

Semi outdoor lounge on middle level   中間階の半屋外ラウンジ

Phase I (left) and II (right)　I期(左)とII期(右)

Swimming pool on middle level　中間階のスイミング・プール

Staircase: view toward sea　階段：遠くに海を望む

Axial staircase　軸となる階段

Rokko Housing II, 1985-93

Unit on 14th floor　S=1:500

△▷ Apartment on 14th floor　14階の住戸

Courtyard on 10th floor　10階の中庭

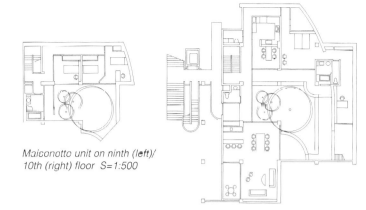
Maisonotto unit on ninth (left)/
10th (right) floor　S=1:500

Apartment on 10th floor (maisonette)　10階の住戸（メゾネット）

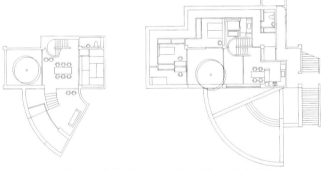
Maisonette unit on sixth (left)/seventh (right) floor　S=1:500

◁△ Apartment on sixth/seventh floor (maisonette)　6，7階の住戸（メゾネット）

103

View from phase II toward III II期よりIII期を見る

△ *View toward swimming pool from roof terrace* ルーフ・テラスよりスイミング・プールを見る
▽ *Court between wings* 棟の間の庭

Rokko Housing III, 1992-99

Interior of apartment 住戸内部

Roof garden of lower wing　低層棟，屋上庭園

Sixth floor

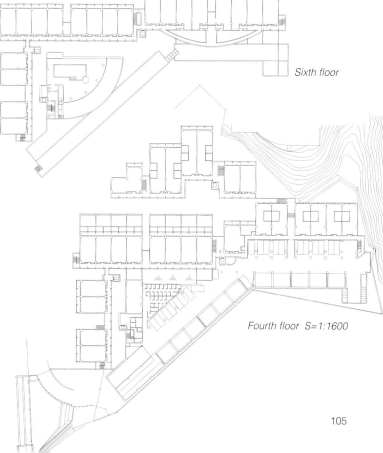
Fourth floor S=1:1600

Terrace of apartment　住戸テラス

1979–80
A DESIGN GROUP
David M. Cooper, Richard Clemenson, Michael W. Folonis

BARRINGTON CONDOMINIUMS
West Los Angeles, California, U.S.A.

Overall view

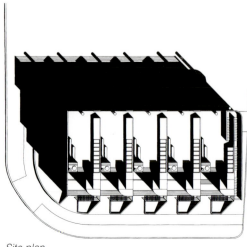

Site plan

The project is located on a major residential street in West Los Angeles. The lot is approximately 56' x 110' (6,160 square feet) and is bounded by two streets, an alley and a single-family residence. The neighborhood consists of a combination single and multiple family dwellings.

The intention of the architect was to satisfy the client (developer) needs for maximizing the number of condominium units at a budget cost of $35.00 per square foot.

Along with economic constraints the architects intended to maximize interior space while allowing ample private exterior decks. The project was to reflect a consideration for the sur-

Partial elevation:
3 stories for one unit above parking on ground level
立面：地上レベルより上3階で1ユニットになっている

rounding neighborhood while maintaining a strong identity of its own. Each unit was to have a separate entrance in close proximity to the garage. Security and unit individuality were other important considerations.

Parking is accessible from the alley at street level. The enclosure for parking is concrete block with chain link gates leading to the individual units. Distances between parking stalls and unit entries is kept to a minimum. The entry stairs, parking gates and planters combine to individualize and separate each unit.

The second level rests on a 12-inch concrete slab supported by the concrete block walls and 3-12 inch concrete columns. The two bedrooms are located on this level. Seclusion from street traffic is achieved by recessing the wall and allowing planter space between window and street.

The third level contains the kitchen and living area. The mezzanine level above covers only 1/3 of the living area which not only stays within code requirements, but opens up the living room space and provides a third story balcony with an attractive view.

The rounded elements serve to identify the entrances and vertical circulation, and provide physical separation between exterior decks.

Skylights are situated to illuminate the stairwells and oriented to minimize solar heat gain. Extension of the skylight frame at the roof allows additional storage space for each unit. Insulated mechanical components are left exposed to maintain the consistency of clear identification of major building elements.

Above the garage level and the concrete slab of the second level, construction is wood frame with stucco exterior and drywall interior.

This project exploits the concept of separation and identification of elements while maintaining a strong sense of unity. It contains exciting spaces and provides an extremely interesting addition to the neighborhood.

View toward kitchen from living room on third floor　3階，居間より台所を見る

Living room　居間

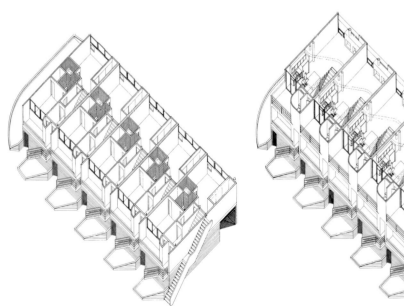
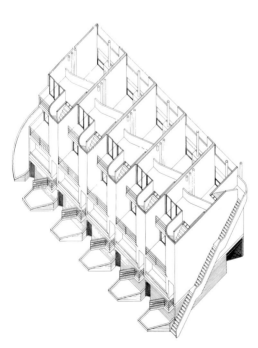
Isometrics

Staircase between third floor and mezzanine　3階と中3階の間の階段

1 ENTRANCE	5 DINING ROOM
2 BEDROOM	6 LIVING ROOM
3 BATHROOM	7 DECK
4 KITCHEN	8 MEZZANINE

Mezzanine

Third floor

Second floor

　これは西ロサンゼルスの高級住宅街に計画された。敷地は約17×34メートル（約570平方メートル）で，そのまわりには2本の街路と1本の小道，および戸建住宅がある。周辺には，戸建住宅や集合住宅が建ち並んでいる。

　設計にあたって建築家の意図は，施主（ディベロッパー）の希望する条件，つまり1平方メートル当り約377ドルの予算内で，この共同管理アパートメントの住戸数を最大限にするということであった。

　経済的制約を踏まえた上で，建築家は内部空間を大きくとろうとした。と同時に，外部のプライベート・デッキも広くとろうと考えた。この計画では，一方で近隣との関係を考慮しながら，それ自身の強い個性を確保しようとする意図があった。それぞれの住戸は，別々の入口を持ち，その入口はガレージに非常に近く置かれている。防犯や各住戸の個別性もまた重要なものとして考慮された。

　駐車場には道路レベルの小道から入ることができる。この駐車場を囲む壁は，コンクリート・ブロックで，そこには各住戸へのワイヤー・メッシュ製の門が据えられている。駐車場と各住戸への入口とは全て最短距離になるようにしている。入口への階段，駐車場の門，植栽，それらによって各住戸を区切り，独立性を与えている。

　2階は約30センチ厚のコンクリートのスラブの上にあり，そのスラブはコンクリート・ブロック壁と，約7.5×30センチのコンクリート柱によって支えられている。二つの寝室がこの階にある。街路からの交通騒音を防ぐために，壁面を街路から後退させ，また街路と窓との間には植栽の場所を設けた。

　3階は台所と居間。中3階は，居間の3分の1程度にかかるが，それは法規制を満たすとともに，居間空間を見下ろし，かつ3階のバルコニーに開き，魅力的な眺望を与える。

　曲面の要素は，各住戸の入口と階段室をそれとはっきりわからせるためだけでなく，各外部デッキを物理的に分けるためでもある。

　トップライトは階段室を明るくし，かつ太陽熱が最小限に抑えられるような位置に置かれている。屋上階ではトップライトのフレームが延長され，その部分は各住戸の予備倉庫にあてられる。また，この階には各機械装置がむき出しのまま個別に置かれているが，それは，この建物の主要な要素を，ここでも個々に表現した結果である。

　ガレージと2階コンクリート・スラブより上は木造で，外部はスタッコ塗り，内部は乾式壁の仕上げになっている。

　この計画は，全体に強い統一感を与えながらも各要素に個別的な表現を与えるという意図を展開したものであり，そして，それ自身魅力的な空間を持ちながら，周囲には大変おもしろい関係を持つものとしてまとまったのである。

1980–84
MANOLO NUÑEZ-YANOWSKY

LES ARÈNES DE PICASSO
Marne-la-Vallée, France

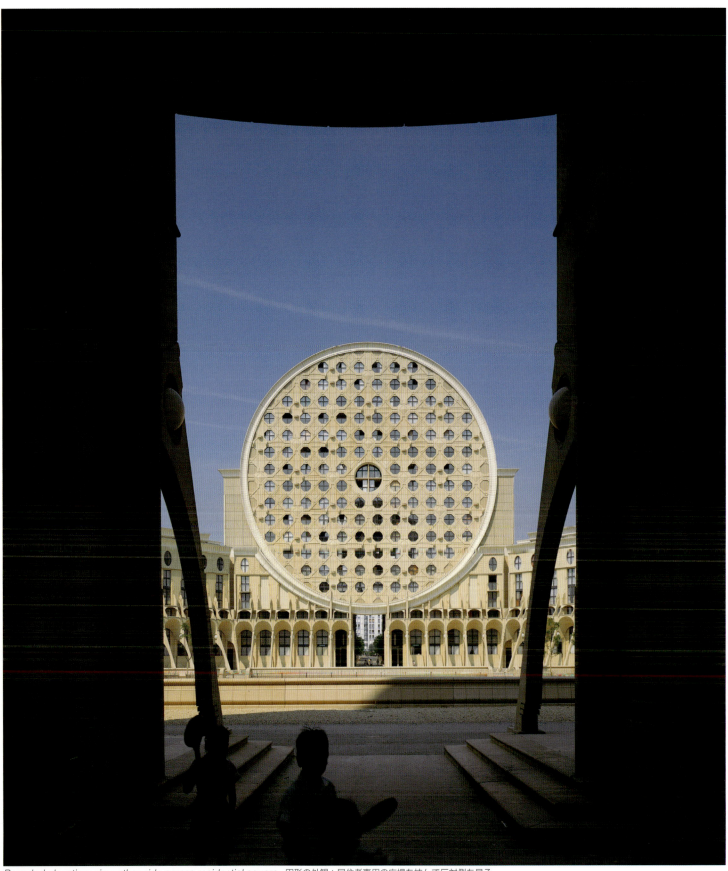

Rounded elevation: view other side across residential square　円形の外観：居住者専用の広場を挟んで反対側を見る

Internal elevation facing residential square 居住者専用の広場に面した外観

The "540 complex" in the center of the Pavée Neuf District in the new town of Marne-la-Vallée was the winning competition entry on the basis of the submitted file in January 1980. The initial program provided for 540 dwelling in two sections, one of 400 dwellings and the other of 140 dwellings, together with the residential communal areas, equipment and 800 m² of shops on the ground floor. The parking facilities for the entire program are built near the square in the form of 3 underground car parks, financed by the EPA.

The competition theme was to design a residential square with a strongly urban character around a central garden.

In view of the tradition followed in the 1960s-1970s by French new town planners who repeatedly used BAUHAUS "zoning" as the basis of any kind of planning or urban development, the task of designing a major urban space was all the more difficult.

We believe that the success of this operation was due essentially to the common purpose shared by the Directorate of New Towns, the Noisy-le-Grand Town Council, the developer FFF and the firm COGIF and, to the frank and generous support which we received from the Ministry of Building, particularly the Building Plan Department. All this help and support enabled us to bring this ambitious experiment to a successful conclusion.

The key image underpinning the project was dream and the fantastic, which was inspired by the fantastic and revolutionary architecture of different periods. By means, of computer design, it was meticulously broken down into 4,700 prefabricated parts, using a highly sophisticated large-unit prefabrication process.

Manolo Nuñez-Yanowsky

111

Distant view 遠景

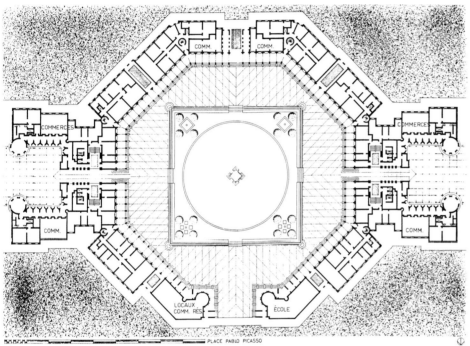
Plan

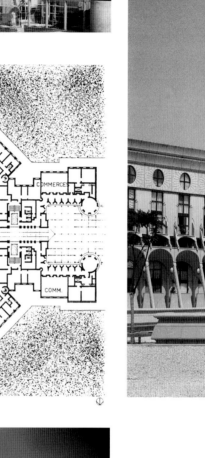

Corridor facing residential square 居住者専用の広場に面した回廊

マルヌ・ラ・ヴァレ・ニュータウンのパヴェ・ヌフ地区中央に立地する540戸のコンプレックスは，1980年1月に提出して入賞した設計競技案に基づいている。当初は140戸と400戸を二つの地区に分けて配置し，居住者が共有する800平米の店舗が1階に設けられる計画であった。全地区に対する駐車施設はEPAの補助を受け広場近くの地下に3層に渡って建設された。

　設計競技のテーマは，住居に付属したきわめて都市的性格の強い広場を，庭園を中心にしてデザインすることであった。あらゆる種類のプランニングや都市開発の基礎にもバウハウス以来の「ゾーニング」を繰り返してきたフランスのニュータウンのプランナーによる1960年代から70年代に続く伝統からすると，メジャーな都市空間をデザインすることはますます困難な状況に立ちいたっていた。

View from residential square 居住者専用の広場から見る

　この計画を成功させるにはまず、ニュータウン計画の管理者、ノワジー・ル・グラン都市議会、デベロッパーFFF、COGIF社に共有できる目的意識を持つこと、そして建設省、特に建築計画局からわれわれが受けたような十分な援助を得ることが必要だと信じる。このような支持や援助によりこの野心的な実験は成功を納めることができた。

　このプロジェクトに織り込まれたキーとなるイメージは、様々な時代の空想的で革命的な建築によって鼓舞された夢とファンタジーである。コンピュータの利用により、それらは微細な4,700のプレファブ・パーツにブレークダウンされ、高度に洗練された大型ユニットのプレファブリケーション化に利用された。

（マノロ・ニュネズ・ヤノヴスキー）

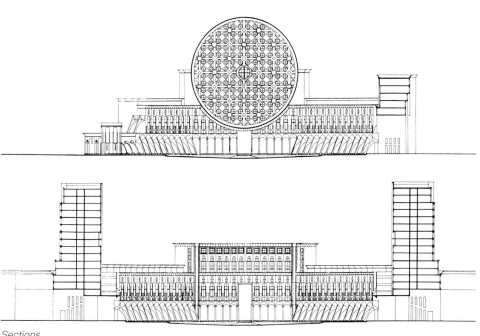

Sections

1982–85
HENRI GAUDIN

HOUSING IN EVRY
Evry, France

Overall view from northeast 北東側全景

I hope that my small number of built forms will give people a feeling of my concerns about space. This is reflected in the will to set volume against volume, so that buildings will not stand, as it were, in the solitude of mere objects.

I divide masses only to bring them closer together. I open them up slightly to provide clearings, I set them apart to play upon their contrasts. It is surely our task to open up the material, to break it, to provide thresholds to make it hospitable, or in all events, to get closer to it.

In this sense, architecture is a kind of weaving together of solid bodies and empty spaces. It involves building relations between walls and streets, relations of volumes with courtyards, making the material breathe, creating an intimate connection between the material and space. The point is that the architect's task is to create places for people to live in.

Habitation necessitates thinking in terms of threshold, positive space, distancing and interruption. Without these aspects, without a form that both encompasses and receives, there can be no dwelling.

It is implicit in this argument that architecture cannot be an object. It can only be manifested as a social fact as a way of forging closer relations with others: houses, trees, the sky. It can exist only as one element of a plurality. The town is a good example of this. It possesses treasures of contrivance and exhibits a remarkable spatial ingenuity. Rather than being an obstacle, the town enriches architectural thought, when the new town is a desert.
Henri Gaudin

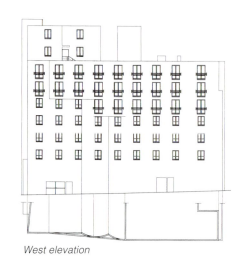

West elevation

私が空間について考えていることを，数少ない私の作品から感じとってもらいたいと願っている。それは，ヴォリュームに対抗してヴォリュームを配置するところに表われている。その結果建物は言わば単なるオブジェとして屹立することはない。

各部分が寄りそっているように見せるためにのみマッスは分割された。透き間をあけるためにマッスはわずかに切開された。マッスのコントラストを楽しむために引き離して配置された。暖かく人を受け入れ，そこで起るすべての出来事へと近づくために，素材を切り開き分割し，境界域をつくり出すことがわれわれの仕事であると確信する。

こう考えるとき，建築はソリッドな実体とヴォイドなスペースとの一種の織物となる。そこには壁と街路の関係性，ヴォリュームと中庭との関係性が含まれる。そして素材が息づき素材と空間との親密な関係が生まれる。建築家の仕事は人々が生活する場所をつくることだという点がポイントである。住まうことは境界域，ポジティヴな空間，距離，中断という用語についての考慮を必要とする。こういった観点や，包みこみ受けとめる空間なくしては，住居は成立し得ない。

この主張には，建築はオブジェではあり得ないことが意味されている。建築は社会的事実なのであり，たとえば住宅，樹木，空など他との関係性の中につくり上げられる。多数の中の一要素として建物は存在するのである。都市はその良い例だ。都市は仕組みの宝庫であり，著しい空間的な独創性を持つ。さまざまな問題を含むにもかかわらず，都市は建築的思考に富むが，ニュータウンは不毛である。

（アンリ・ゴーダン）

Looking northeast from walkway on upper level 上階の通路より北東を見る

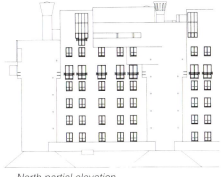

North partial elevation

South elevation

Section

Looking east from walkway on upper level 上階の通路より東を見る

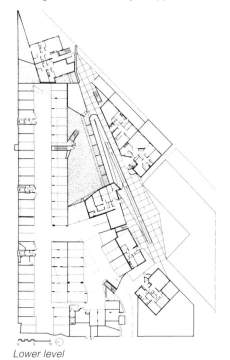

Lower level

Upper level

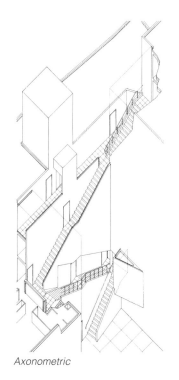

Axonometric

View from east 東より見る

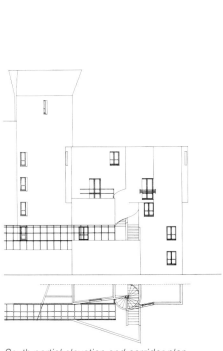

South partial elevation and corridor plan

Looking west from connecting corridor 渡り廊下より西を見る

1983–86
HENRI E. CIRIANI

LOGNES
Marne-la-Vallée, France

Looking northeast 北東を見る

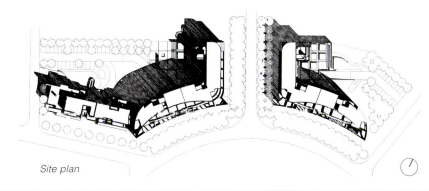

Site plan

Looking north 北を見る

The project is situated at the edge (boundary) of a development in a district of the new town of Marne-la-Vallée, opposite an elevation resulting from construction work carried out locally which now serves as a protective embankment for the nearby motorway. This raised area has been turned into a sports and leisure park.

The southerly crescent shape imposed on it is intersected by a road linking the park to the central area, the flat area where the development is interspersed with artificial lakes.

This tight curve is clearly intersected in the middle, which led us to work with the idea of a building on three parallel levels:
- the first adapting itself to the perimeter of the land (a lattice level whose height corresponds with that of the upper terrace level of the park) and which functions as a commercial arcade on the ground floor;
- the second, straight, delineating the habitable boundary of the apartments behind the grid (with terraced balconies bridging the gap between these two levels);
- the third, consisting of the two upper levels which have a pronounced curve, with the aim of making the two structures on either side of the road more independent of one another, and at the same time having the effect of "stretching" the composition outwards and of anchoring the spaces in the center, behind the lattice. This opaque fixity makes it possible for the first level to "blend" with the space in front of it.

The superimposed terrace treatment, resembling wings which are torn away from the first grid, also serves the purpose of appearing to bring together the two sides of the central axis.

At the angle in the building, two porches face each other, thereby creating a dynamic feature perpendicular to the dynamics of the central axis, integrating the width of that axis. These porches form an access area for the residential parts of the building. From this area, the vertical circulations of the entrance halls (three to each arm of the building) lead off. The building is crowned with a roof-top maisonette typology, these maisonettes being reached by a "street in the air" looking out over the whole of the new town.

This "rear" face of the building is treated with more massive proportions so as to "anchor" its convexity and to give the work the effect of a larger scale, bearing in mind that the building can be seen from a considerable distance at this point.

A lower building is to be grafted onto the west side of the main construction. While it blends in with the morphology of the latter, it is different in that it has its own separate central distribution system: a single well, open vertically on all its five floors and crossed by horizontal passageways—closed in behind a north-facing curtain wall—running along two-thirds of the length of the building. The different design of this building was dictated by the building program. The apartments in this building are for sale, whereas the others are for letting.

Since, according to the specifications for the new town, this building is to be the focal point of the new district, it is the first one built and the highest. It serves as a reference point for the subsequent building work, in terms of both character and color.

Constructed from concrete shells over a 5.60 meters grid, the building exhibits three different types of joinery: joinery painted racing-green for the large openings of the apartments close to the center, white plastic for the small openings on the exposed exterior, and fine metalwork for the common areas. All horizontal surfaces (the wall copings, window ledges, low walls, etc.) are covered with white tiles, as the vertical surfaces of the commercial arcade (height 2 meters). The concrete shells are surfaced with marble chippings, which afford a good overall uniformity of appearance.
Henri E. Ciriani

Overall view of east building: view from south 東棟全景：南より見る

Overall view of east building: view from southwest 東棟全景：南西より見る

敷地はマルヌ・ラ・ヴァレ・ニュータウンの外れにあり，近くで行われた建設工事によって生じた盛土による台地（今は，高速道路の遮音壁として役立っている）に面している。この台地はスポーツ／レジャー・パークへと変身した。

建物は南を向いた半月形で，公園と人工湖を掘り開発が進行中のニュータウンの平坦な中央部とを結ぶ道路で分断されている。

この細身の半月形のちょうど真中を道路が貫通していることから，平行する三つの層で建物を構成することにした。

第1層。敷地境界に沿い，格子状の構成で，公園の上部テラス・レベルと高さをそろえ，1階の店舗のアーケードとして機能する。

第2層。直線状で第1層の格子層の背後で居住部を構成する。第1層と第2層の間隙をバルコニーが結んでいる。

第3層。非常に目立つ曲線をもった最上部2層を収め，この強い曲線によって，中央の道路によって分断された二つの棟をお互い独立したものとして見せると同時に，建物を外側に「引き伸ばし」，第1層の格子の背後の空間をしっかりと固定させる効果をもたせることを狙っている。この不透明な第3層でしっかりと固定することで，1階をその前にひろがるスペースと「とけ合わせる」ことも可能なのである。

第1層と第2層の間に積層するバルコニーは，

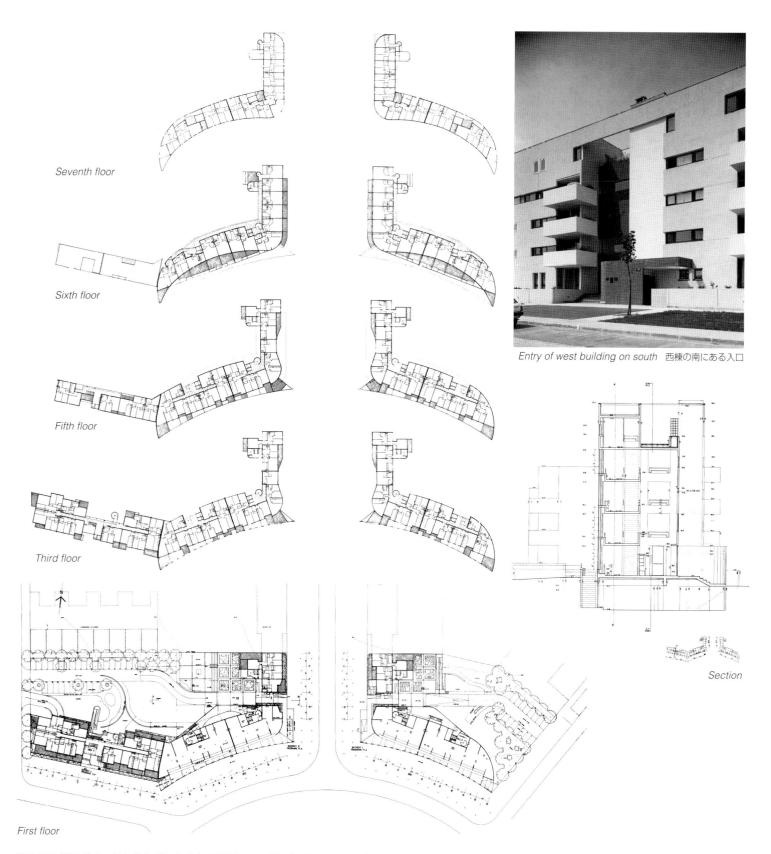

Seventh floor

Sixth floor

Fifth floor

Third floor

First floor

Entry of west building on south 西棟の南にある入口

Section

　第1層の格子グリッドからちぎり取られた翼棟のようでもあり，両側を一つにまとめる働きもしている。

　建物北側の角で，ポーチが二つ向き合っている。これによって，中央軸をはさむ両側を統合し，その軸線の動きに対し垂直方向の力学をつくり出している。これらのポーチは住戸へのアクセス・エリアを構成する。ここから入口ホール（全体で3箇所）の垂直のサーキュレーションが始まる。最上階はメゾネット住戸で，「空中道路」がひろがり，ニュータウン全体を見晴らせる。

　建物の背面には，どっしりとしたプロポーションをもたせた。凸面状の建物を大地に「つなぎ」とめる大きなスケール感を与えるためである。はるか遠くからでもこの建物を認めることができるようにすることを心にとめていた。

　主屋の西側に低層の建物が継ぎ足されている。主屋に用いた形態言語を混合してはいるが，この建物は独自の動線システムをもっている。一つの吹き抜けに面して5層それぞれが開かれ，北面するカーテンウォールで覆われた建物の3分の2の長さの通路が，吹き抜けを横断する。主屋とデザインを変えたのは，前者が賃貸用，こちらは分譲用というプログラム上の相異による。

　ニュータウンの設計仕様書によれば，この建物は，この新しい開発地区の焦点となり，最初に建設され，最も高層のものとなり，建物の性格，色彩の点で，これに続く建物の参考になるものとされていた。

　建物は5.60メートルグリッドのコンクリート・シェル造で，3種類の建具を用いている。中央部に近い住戸の，大きな開口の窓枠は緑色。外側に向いた小さな開口は白いプラスチック，共有エリアには金属を用いている。水平要素（壁の笠石，窓の棚板，腰壁，他）はすべて白タイル貼り，2メートル高のアーケードも同様である。コンクリート・シェルには大理石の細片を混ぜたものを仕上げに使い，外観上の全体の統一感を生み出した。

（アンリ・シリアニ）

1985–87
JEAN NOUVEL

NEMAUSUS I
Nîmes, France

Overall view of building B: view from east　B棟全景：東より見る

View of top level 最上階を見る

Looking west from pathway on top level. Building A on right 最上階の通路より西を見る。右はA棟

This public housing project in Nîmes in the south of France, has a total floor area of 10,300 square meters. There are 114 units of three kinds—simplex, duplex, and triplex—and 17 types. Each unit faces both south and north and is flanked by a 3-meter wide balcony. The north balcony is used for circulation, and the south as a terrace. There is no partition between dining room and kitchen, and the result is a spacious interior. The walls and ceiling are exposed concrete. The stairs and catwalks are of perforated aluminum, and the floor is finished in a gray plastic. The door to the south terrace is a garage door. Abstract wall paintings were done by an artist to cover up damaged areas on the wall and help to soften the overall effect. The designer's intention was "to depart from the general character of past public housing; i.e. the cramped spaces, exposure only on one side; and narrow terraces."

Corner of building A　A棟角部

Entrance of each unit　各住戸のエントランス

Duplex unit　デュプレックス・タイプの住戸

Duplex unit on east end　東端のデュプレックス・タイプの住戸

南仏ニーム市に建つ公共集合住宅。延床面積10,300平米。シンプレックス，デュプレックス，トリプレックスからなる3種17タイプの住戸114ユニットを収容。各戸は南北両方向に面し，どちらにも3メートル幅の広いバルコニーが廻っている。北側のバルコニーはサーキュレーション，南側のバルコニーはテラスとして使われる。食堂と台所の間仕切はなく，広い室内空間を生みだしている。壁と天井は打放しコンクリート。有孔アルミニウム製の階段とキャットウォーク。床は灰色のプラスティック貼り。南面するテラスに開いた扉はガレージ用のものである。打放しコンクリートの壁の傷跡にはアーティストの協力で抽象的な壁画が描かれ，荒々しい感じを和らげている。設計者の意図：「従来の公共集合住宅の一般的性格 — 狭い空間，一方向のみに開いた開口，狭いテラス — を一新すること」。

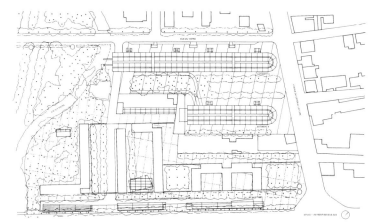

1 ENTRANCE
2 LIVING ROOM
3 KITCHEN/DINING ROOM
4 BEDROOM
5 BATHROOM
6 TERRACE

Site plan

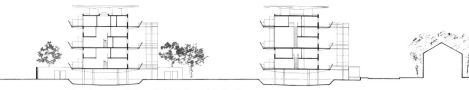

Sections: building A (right) and B (left)

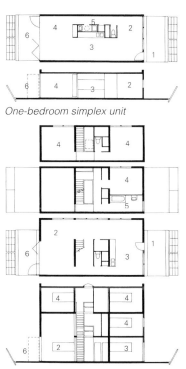

One-bedroom simplex unit

Three-bedroom triplex unit

Plan and section: four-bedroom duplex unit

Looking southwest: building B on left and courtyard on right　南西を見る：左はB棟，右は中庭

1988–91
RENZO PIANO

RUE DE MEAUX HOUSING
Paris, France

Garden 庭

Southeast garden elevation　南東庭側の外観

Louvers　ルーバー

Central Garden for All Residents

This is the main idea in designing this building which is located in a densely populated area of the 19th arrondissement in Paris. The building, with a general rectangular shape, can be thought of as a mass built to fit into the existing urban fabric on its outside perimeter while its center has been "carved out" to accommodate an interior green space. Two narrow "slots" divide the constructions in three sections on the street side, with just a glimpse towards the garden. The contrast between the bustle of the street and the calm of the garden created an effect of surprise for the residents who must walk through the garden to reach their building entrance. Landscaping includes low shrubbery and spinney of sliver birchwood.

Great Diversity of Apartments

The volumetric diversity of the building results in a wide variety of apartments. However, for the buildings bordering the garden and for the blocks on the east and west separated by the slots, model apartments with fairly neutral and flexible layouts were created. Essentially they comprise a large crosswise room facing north and south with a balcony or winter garden at either end; a conventional "night" area is adjacent. Therefore each apartment of the 220 created, has two exposures: the garden and the urban neighborhood.

Facades onto the Interior Garden:

The upper stories (levels 2-7), are made of prefabricated GRC elements (glass fiber reinforced concrete) which form a primary projecting frame about five centimeters thick and 30 centimeters deep on a 90- by 90-centimeter grid (approximately). The framework thus defined is filled either with opaque, insulating elements covered in natural tone terra cotta plates (20- by 42-centimeter modules), or with GRC screen elements. In the latter case, the framework is white.

For these facades the architectural impression derives from the geometrical strictness, unity of materials and the richness of their textures. On levels 0 and 1, also on the garden, glass elements (surface treated to ensure privacy) are fitted in the same frames used for the terra cotta elements. These facades correspond to two-story volumes (apartment-studio workshop).

Continuous Vertical Facades on Street Side and Outfacing Exteriors:

The materials and grid outlines are identical, but the facades do not project from the primary structure. The facade is more "calm" while retaining the same richness of materials.

Facades on Extremities:

The third type concerns the facades on the receding parts of the series of balconies on the two longitudinal blocks. Partially cut on an oblique angle (see section), the volumes are covered in colored enamel panels In addition, the sun protection elements provided here are supported by a light steel framework, inclined at 45 degrees in accordance with building outline regulations.

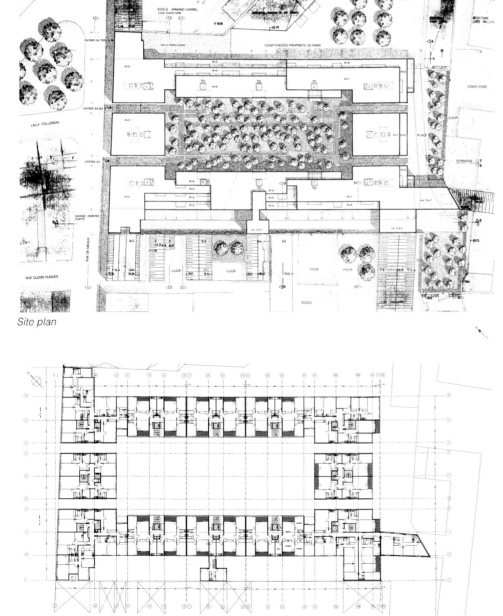

Site plan

Typical floor

Northeast garden elevation 北東庭側の外観

Garden elevation/section (2)

Elevation on rue de Meaux (1)

Garden elevation/section (6)

Southwest elevation/section (5)

居住者全員のための中庭

これがパリ19区の人口密度の高い地域に位置する，このハウジング・デザインの中心テーマである。ごく普通の長方形の建物は，内側に緑地をとるために中央部を切り取られている一方，外周沿いの都市ファブリックに合わせて建てられた一つのマッスとも考えられる。道路側では，二つの細い「スロット」が建物を3分割し，そのスロットを通して中庭が垣間見える。通りの喧噪と庭の静かさとの対比が，その庭を歩いて建物玄関へ進むことになる居住者に意外性を感じさせる。庭には背の低い潅木やすらりとしたカバの木が植えられている。

多様性のある住戸

建物の容積が不規則であるために，各戸は変化に富んだものとなった。しかし，中庭に面した棟やスロットで切り離された東側と西側の棟は，適度にニュートラルで柔軟性のある室内構成になっている。基本的には，南北両側に面していて，その両端（片側が平凡な「夜」の繁華街に隣接している）にバルコニーかウィンターガーデンのある，広い細長い部屋で構成される。つまり220ある住戸はそれぞれ，庭と市街の両方に面することになる。

中庭に面したファサード

上階（レベル2～7）はGRC（グラスファイバー強化セメント）造のプレファブ部材でつくられている。これは約90センチ角グリッドに載った，約5センチ厚，奥行さ30センチの最も突出した部分のフレームを構成する。このように規定されたフレームワークは，自然色のテラコッタ・プレート（20×42センチモデュール）で覆われた不透明の断熱のエレメントか，あるいはGRCスクリーンのエレメントで充填される。後者の場合はフレームは白である。

これらのファサードでは，その精密な幾何学的規律性，材料とその豊かなテクスチャーによって建築的な表情が生まれている。同じ中庭側の地上階と2階では，ガラス（プライバシー保護のために表面処理がされている）が，テラコッタを充填しているのと同じタイプのフレームにはめ込まれている。これらのファサードは2層吹抜けの部分（アパートメント＝スタジオ・ワークショップ）に対応している。

道路側ファサードと敷地外に面する外壁

材料とグリッドの組立は中庭側と同じだが，ファサードは主要な構造体から突き出していない。材料の豊かさは変わらないが，その表情は中庭側より静かである。

端部のファサード

三つ目のタイプは横長の二つのブロックに連続して設置されているバルコニーの後退部のファサードである。これらは部分的に斜めに切り取られ（断面参照），エナメル塗りのカラーパネルで披覆されている。また，ここで使われている日除けは，建築の外形規制に従って45度傾けた，軽量鉄骨フレームによって支持されている。

1988–91
RIKEN YAMAMOTO

HODAKUBO HOUSING
Kumamoto, Japan

Overall view from south　南側全景

1 COMMUNITY ROOM   *Site plan S=1:2000*

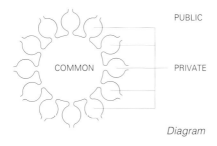

Diagram

It is a 110 units housing complex.

The most distinct point about this project from ordinary housing developments should be the central-garden-type site plan that 110 units surround the central open space. 31 units out of 110 units are distributed to the west side of the open space, 30 units to the north side and 49 units to the east side. A community room is located on the south side. That is, all four sides of the central open space are completely enclosed with the three, west, north and east buildings and the community room. What is further unique is that no gate is equipped to directly enter the open space. It is not designed for anyone to freely enter the open space. In other words, the open space is closed toward the outside and is made with a mechanism to be exclusive for the people living in the housing complex.

The mechanism is shown in Diagram. Each unit plays a role as a threshold to the central open space.

The reason for the closure is from a consideration that the open space should belong above all to the residents. Furthermore, each unit does not at all need to be protective against the open space, because the residents belong to the space. It is a simple ratio-

View from street on west 西側道路より見る

nale that the units surrounding the open space can be wide-open to the space to the degree it is closed to the outside. Therefore, living space in each unit is made exposed toward the open space as much as possible. Large openings and a wide terrace are also open toward the open space.

On the contrary, private rooms are arranged on the side of a road and made to intercept glances from the outside to the extent possible. Further, the private rooms and living rooms are located in separate buildings and both are connected by a bridge on the third to fifth floor and by a small courtyard on the second floor. The entire site plan and each unit plan are all decided in the mechanism of the closed-off open space.

To add some more, an entrance to outside is actually furnished next to the community room. The decision for the door to be closed all the time, only at night or to be open only at the time of regional festival should be decided by the residents of the housing complex. It is to mean that closed toward outside is an aspect of architectural mechanism and how the residents use it is another.

Riken Yamamoto

110戸の集合住宅である。

従来の集合住宅の計画と最も異なる点は，この110戸の住宅が中心の広場を囲む，囲み庭型の配置計画になっている点ではないかと思う。110戸の住戸は中央広場を中心にして，広場の西側に31戸，北側に30戸，東側に49戸がそれぞれ配置されている。南側には集会室がある。つまりこの中央広場は西棟，北棟，東棟の三つの棟，それと集会室によって，完全に四方を囲まれているわけである。さらに特徴的なのは，この広場に直接入るためのゲートのようなものを特に準備していないという点である。外から誰でも自由にこの広場に入ってくることができる，というようにはでき上がっていないのである。つまり，外部に対して閉鎖的にできている。この集合住宅に住む人たちの専用であるようなメカニズムになっているのである。

West elevation facing court　中庭側西面

　そのメカニズムを図示すればダイアグラム（p.131）のようになる。各住戸が中央の広場に対する閾（threshold）の役割を果たしているわけである。
　閉鎖的である理由は，この広場が何よりもまず，この集合住宅に住んでいる人々にこそ帰属すべきだと考えたからである。そして，住人たちに帰属する広場だからこそ，各住戸はその広場に対して防御的になる必要はまったくないということになる。広場が外部に対して閉鎖的な分だけ，その広場を巡る住戸は，逆に広場に対して開放的にすることができるという単純な理由である。だから，各住戸の居間部分は広場に対しては可能なかぎり開放的にできている。大きな開口も広いテラスも広場の方に向かって開いている。
　反対にループ状の道の側に配置されている個室部分は，なるべく外からの視線を遮るようにできている。そしてその個室部分と居間部分とが分棟になっていて，両者を3〜5階ではブリッジが，そして2階では小さな中庭が結びつけているわけである。全体の配置計画も各住戸の平面計画も，すべての計画はこの閉鎖的な広場のメカニズムによって決定されているというような計画である。
　付け加えておけば，広場が外部に対して閉鎖的であるといっても，実際には集会室の横に外部への出入口が準備されている。このドアが常に閉められているのか，あるいは夜間だけ閉められるのか，あるいはお祭りのときに周辺に開放されるのか，それはこの集合住宅に住んでいる人々の意思によって決定されるべきことだと思う。外部に対して閉鎖的だというのは建築のメカニズムの話である。そのメカニズムを住民たちがどう利用するかは，また別の問題だという意味である。

（山本理顕）

Site

Apartment on top floor with arched roof　アーチ型の屋根の架かる最上階

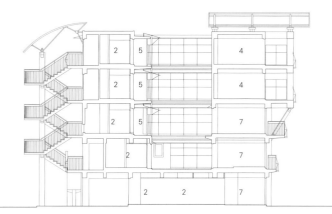
Section　S=1:300

Community room for residents　集会室

Court: looking sourth. Community room for residents on center
中庭：南を見る。正面は集会室

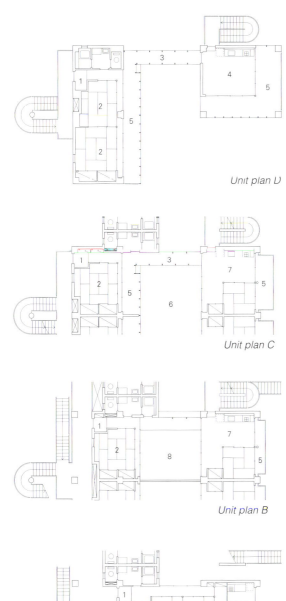

Unit plan D

Unit plan C

Unit plan B

Unit plan A S=1:300

1 ENTRANCE
2 PRIVATE ROOM
3 BRIDGE
4 LIVING-DINING-KITCHEN
5 TERRACE
6 VOID
7 DINING-KITCHEN
8 COURT

Interior of apartment: view toward living/dining/kitchen through court
住戸内部：中庭越しに居間／食堂／台所を見る

Bridge on top floor　最上階，渡り廊下

1989–91
STEVEN HOLL

VOID SPACE/HINGED SPACE HOUSING
Fukuoka, Japan

Overall view from south 南側全景

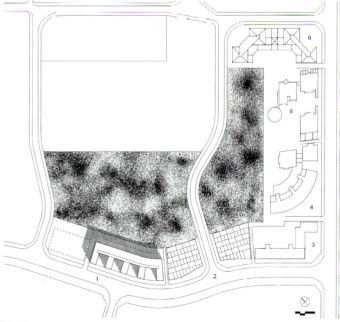

1 Steven Holl
2 Rem Koolhaas
3 Mark Mack
4 Osamu Ishiyama
5 Christian de Portzamparc
6 Oscar Tusquets

Site plan

Concept:
From hinged space to the silence of void space

Four active north-facing voids interlock with four quiet south-facing voids to bring a sense of the sacred into direct contact with everyday, domestic life. To ensure emptiness, the south voids are flooded with water; the sun makes flickering reflections across the ceilings of the north courts and apartment interiors.

Interiors of the 28 apartments revolve around the concept of "hinged space," a development of the multi-use concepts of traditional Fusuma taken into an entirely modern

Water court on second floor 2階，水庭

dimension. One type of hinging–diurnal–allows an expansion of the living area during the day, reclaimed for bedrooms at night. Another type–episodic–reflects the change in a family over time; rooms can be added or subtracted to accommodate grown children leaving the family or elderly parents moving in.

An experiential sense of passage through space is heightened in the three types of access, which allow apartments to have exterior front doors. On the lower passage, views across the water court and through the north voids activate the walk spatially from side to side. Along the north passage one has a sense of suspension with the park in the distance. The top passage has a sky view under direct sunlight.

The apartments interlock in section like a complex Chinese box. Individuation from the standpoint of the individual inhabitant has an aim in making all 28 apartments different. Due to the voids and interlocking section, each apartment has many exposures: north, south, east and west.

The structure of exposed bearing concrete is stained in some places. A lightweight aluminum curtain wall allows a reading of the building section while walking from east to west along the street; an entirely different facade of solids is exposed walking from west to east.

The building, with its street-aligned shops and intentionally simple facades, is seen as part of a city in its effort to form space rather than become an architecture of object. Space is its medium, from urban to private, hinged space.

View from north 北より見る

Entrance hall エントランス・ホール

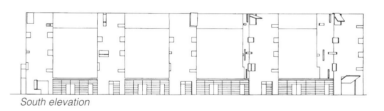
South elevation

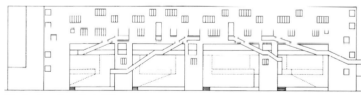
North elevation S=1:800

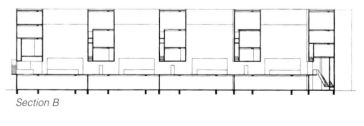
Section B

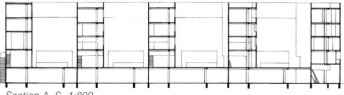
Section A S=1:800

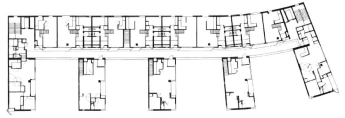
Fifth floor

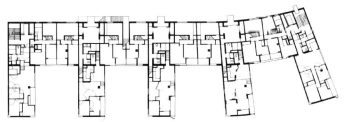
Fourth floor

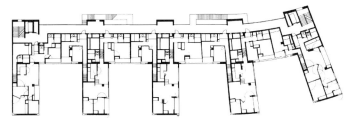
Third floor

Second floor

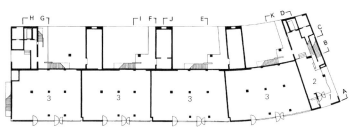
First floor S=1:800

1 MAIN ENTRANCE
2 ENTRANCE HALL
3 COMMERCIAL
4 WATER COURT
5 PASSAGE
6 VOID

コンセプト:
ヒンジのつくる空間から吹抜けの静寂まで

南と北の両側にそれぞれ四つの吹き抜けがある。北側は動的で南側は静的な性格を持ち，それらをかみ合わせることで，日々の家庭生活と神聖な感覚を直接に結びつけようとした。空間が何もないままに守られるよう，南側の吹抜けの下のスラブには水を張る。ここに反射したきらめく光は，北の吹抜けの天井やアパートメントの室内の天井にまで届く。

28戸のアパートメントは，「転換する空間／ヒンジド・スペース」というコンセプトを軸に展開する。これは，日本の伝統的な襖の多用途のコンセプトを現代的な次元に高めたものである。転換の第1の形式 ── 毎日の ── は，日中には生活空間を広くして，夜には一部を寝室に改めるというものだ。次の形式 ── 時々起こる ── は，家族の変化への対応である。成人した子供たちが家を出たり，逆に年老いた親などがやって来たりするのに応じて，部屋数を増やしたり減らしたりすることができる。

三つのタイプが設けられたアクセスルートを通ってゆくと，空間の中をめぐってきたという実感が高められるし，このルートのおかげで，各戸には直接外に面した玄関がつけられる。下の廊下を歩けば，水の中庭ごしの景観と吹抜けを間にした北の景色が眺められるので，空間は生き生きとしたものになる。北側沿いの廊下を歩くと，遠くの公園と一緒に宙に浮かぶような思いにとらわれるし，最上階の廊下に立てば，陽を浴びながら空を眺められるのだ。住戸はさながら複雑なパズルのように断面がかみ合う。それぞれの住人の立場に立って個性を守るために28戸のアパートメント全てを違うものにしようという目的があった。吹抜けと組み合わせる断面のおかげで，どのアパートメントにも数多くの開口が可能になった。北にも南にも，そして東も西も。

打放しコンクリートの構造体は，所々ステインを塗ってある。道を東から西へ歩いて建物を見ると，軽量のアルミのカーテンウォールによって構造体の断面の形を読みとることができる。逆に，西から東に向って歩くと，それぞれに全く違ったファサードが見えてくる。

道路に面して店舗を並べ，ファサードをあえて単純なものにしたことで，建築が都市の一部として感じられる。それは，オブジェとしての建築ではなく，スペースをつくることを意図したからに他ならない。空間とは，都市とひとりの人間の間にあって両者を結ぶヒンジのような媒体(メディア)なのだ。

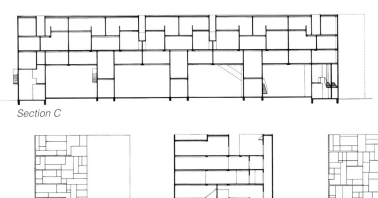
Section C

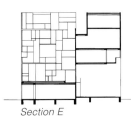
West elevation　*Section D*

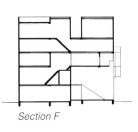
Section E　*Section F*

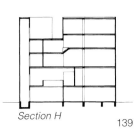
Section H

Entrance hall エントランス・ホール

Interior of unit 住戸内部

Living room 居間

Cabinet キャビネット

Entrance hall 玄関ホール

Entrance 玄関

1989–91
REM KOOLHAAS / OMA
NEXUS WORLD HOUSING
Fukuoka, Japan

Aerial view: Rem wing (center) and Koolhaas wing (right). Steven Holl wing on left (pp.136-141)
上空から見る：レム棟（中央）とコールハース棟（右）。左はスティーヴン・ホール棟 (pp.136-141)

View of Koolhaas wing from northwest street 北西の道路よりコールハース棟を見る

Living (left) and roof terrace (right) 居間（左）とルーフ・テラス（右）

View toward living room from roof terrace ルーフ・テラスより居間を見る

Circumference closed by external wall, lighting through vertical courtyard penetrated each units　周囲は外壁で閉じられ，各住戸を垂直に貫通する中庭から採光する

View toward dining room　食堂を見る

View toward living room　居間を見る

1. Steven Holl
2. Rem Koolhaas
3. Mark Mack
4. Osamu Ishiyama
5. Christian de Portzamparc
6. Oscar Tusquets

Site plan

Lead by the coordinatior, Arata Isozaki, who gathered six architects from around the world, Nexus World was built in a new coastal uptown development area located about seven kilometers north of the central district of Fukuoka. Each architect is given about 40 meter by 40 meter square site, separated by an internal block path. OMA-block is consisted of two 3-storey buildings.

On the south side, the first floor facing the main street is a tall tenant space. On the north side, basing on a half-buried parking as an artificial ground, 3-layered housing units, total of 3 x 4 =12 units (24 units in the both buildings), gather and create a plan composition of a quasi-townhouse without directionality. Naturally, since outer circumferences of units come in contact with other units, each room is configured around a courtyard that penetrates the 3 layers. Masonry-molded black concrete wall covers not only within plans but also the building as a whole. The external appearance was intended to serve as a foot of Isozaki-designed twin towers, considering the situation between

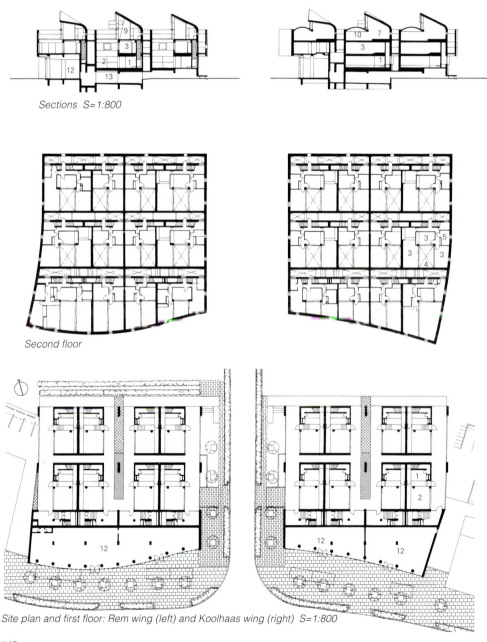

Sections S=1:800

Second floor

Site plan and first floor: Rem wing (left) and Koolhaas wing (right) S=1:800

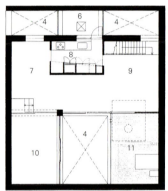

Top level

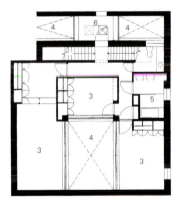

Middle level

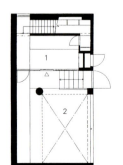

1 ENTRANCE
2 COURTYARD
3 BEDROOM
4 VOID
5 BATHROOM
6 BALCONY
7 DINING ROOM
8 KITCHEN
9 LIVING ROOM
10 STUDY
11 ROOF TERRACE
12 SHOP
13 PARKING

Typical unit plan: lower level S=1:250

an orderly European-style master plan and a Japanese context that Isozaki's 120 meter high twin towers, planned to be erected on both sides of a street similarly to OMA-block, will be adjacently built on the north side in the second phase. (The twin towers were not realized due to the collapsed bubble economy.)

The first layer provides a 3 meter wide road-like slope, or a concourse, which fills a level gap from the parking and functions as an approach to each unit. Only the entrance and the bottom of the courtyards, front yards and spot yards, are placed on the first layer, where urban space and residential space intersect. Each unit, stretching upward from there, is consisted of bedrooms surrounding the courtyard on the second layer and a living room, a dining room and a terrace on the third layer. Largely turning over toward the south, winding roof covers over the living and dining rooms. It creates an impressive urban skyline, or an urban form, in the middle-height cityscape.

View toward dining room from study　書斎より食堂を見る

福岡の旧市街から北に7キロほど離れた，湾岸の新都心開発地で，建築家・磯崎新コーディネートの下，国内外の建築家6人が参加した集合住宅群「ネクサスワールド」。ブロック内道路を挟んだ，それぞれ40メートル角ほどの敷地が割り当てられ，OMA棟は3階建ての建築二つで構成される。

南側のメインストリートに面した1階は天井の高いテナントスペースに当てられ，その北側に半地下の駐車場を人工地盤状にして，3層構成の住戸が，3×4＝12戸（2棟で計24戸）集まった，方向性のないタウンハウスのような平面構成を持つ。当然，住戸外周は他の住戸に接するため，3層を貫く中庭を中心に諸室が配される。平面内だけでなく建物全体としても，石積みを型取りした黒いコンクリート壁で覆われる。整然としたヨーロッパ型マスタープランと，2期として計画されていた，OMA棟同様，道路の両側に建つ磯崎設計のツインタワー（高さ120メートル）が北に隣接するという日本的コンテクストの狭間で，磯崎棟の足元となることを意図した外観だった（ツインタワーはバブル崩壊で実現せず）。

1層部分は，駐車場のレベル差を吸収する，幅3メートルの道路的なスロープ＝コンコースが各住戸までのアプローチとなり，玄関と中庭の底＝前庭・坪庭だけが配され，都市空間と住戸空間が交差する。そこから上方に伸びる各住戸は，2層に中庭を囲んだ寝室，3層に居間・食堂とテラスという構成。居間・食堂には，南に向かって大きくめくれ上がり，うねる屋根が掛かる。それが中層の町並みの中で，印象的な都市のスカイライン＝都市の形をつくり出す。

Courtyard　中庭

1991–96
FRANK O. GEHRY

GOLDSTEIN-SUD HOUSING DEVELOPMENT
Frankfurt, Germany

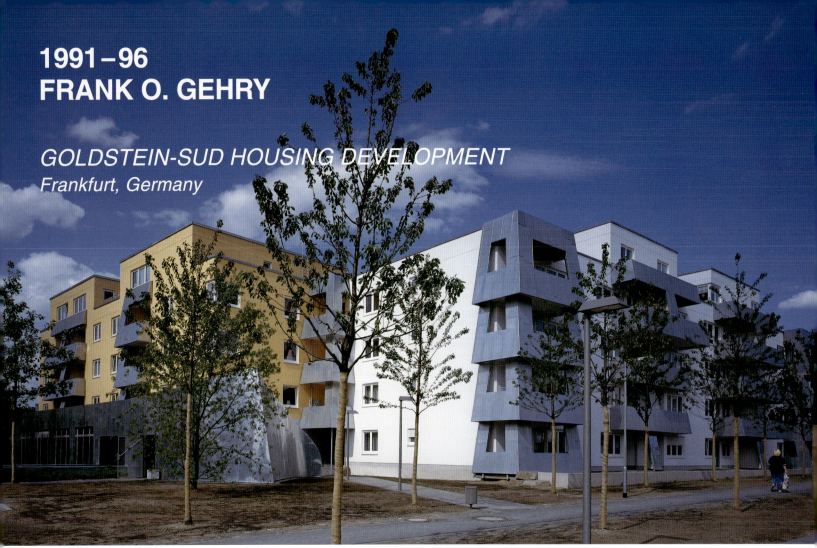

Block 1 (left) and 2 (right) ブロック1（左），2（右）

West elevation of Block 1: entrance to garage on left ブロック1西側壁面：左はガレージ入口

Block 1: west elevation

Block 3: view from court　ブロック3：中庭より見る

Block 4 (left) and 3 (right)　ブロック4（左）と3（右）

The project is located approximately eight kilometers west of downtown Frankfurt at the eastern edge of a public housing zone known as Goldstein South. The site is the last undeveloped public housing tract in the area and provides connections to a community sports field, a future tram stop, and educational facilities. Its position just north of the 'Green belt and south of the neighborhood center and Goldstein Park creates a unique opportunity to integrate with the community.

The program comprises a semi-public park and 162 units of housing with related parking areas, a social center and neighborhood retail. The concept for this site plan was to distribute the park along the natural circulation paths for use by the community. The north/south axis connects the Goldstein Park with the Greenbelt, thereby serving social and recreational needs. The east/west axis connects the Goldstein South housing with the future tram stop and educational facilities thereby serving these daily transportation needs. These two paths are recognizable by their district type of landscape materials and configuration. The north/south recreational path is planted with a variety of trees to create a natural setting connecting the park and the Greenbelt. This community circulation path is also activated by seating and play areas. The east/west transportation path is organized within a linear grid of flowering trees with hardscape paths that accommodate frequent bicycle travel. This path also connects the social center, kindergarten, youth center and sports field.

The apartment blocks are organized in a manner that emphasizes the natural circulation axes while creating partially enclosed courtyards. These courtyards are further subdivided by paths, terraces and private gardens to provide a variety of spaces. The north courtyard uses the metaphor of a tree-lined stream cutting through the earth to create a path for circulation. As the path enters the south courtyard, is splits to reveal a theater shaped space with perimeter seating areas and a sloped grass floor oriented toward the Greenbelt. The buildings conform to the conventional masonry construction systems and materials used by the client (a semi-publicly owned design and development firm). The building aesthetic is derived through the building forms which emphasize entries, stairs, penthouses and balconies. These forms are accented with zinc panels while boldly colored plaster facades comprise the major surface material.

Section

Unit plans

このプロジェクトは，フランクフルトのダウンタウンの西約8キロにある，ゴールドシュタイン・サウスとして知られる公共集合住宅地区の東端に位置している。この敷地は，この地区で最後に残された未開発の公共集合住宅用地で，地域の運動場，将来の市街電車の停車場，教育施設との接続地点となる。緑地帯のすぐ北，都市センターとゴールドシュタイン公園の南という位置は，このコミュニティを統合するのに恰好の場所である。

プログラムには，半公共的な公園，駐車場付きの162戸からなる集合住宅，ソーシャル・センター，店舗が含まれている。この敷地計画に対するコンセプトは，コミュニティでつかわれる自然のままの動線通路に沿って公園を配置するというものである。南北軸はゴールドシュタイン公園と緑地帯を結び，これによって，社会的な，そしてレクリエーションのための必要に応える。東西軸はゴールドシュタイン・サウス集合住宅を将来のトラムの停車場，教育施設と結ぶことによって，日常の交通上の必要に応える。二つの通路は，ランドスケープの材料と構成の違いによって見分けられる。南北のレクリエーション用の道には，公園や緑地帯に続く自然風景をつくるためにさまざまな木々が植えられる。このコミュニティのための通路はまた，ベンチや遊び場で活気づけられる。東西の交通用の道は，頻繁に往来する自転車用の道の付いた，花の咲く樹木のリニアなグリッドで構成されている。この道はまたソーシャル・センター，幼稚園，ユース・センター，運動場とも結ばれる。

アパートメント・ブロックは，部分的に囲まれた中庭をつくりだす一方で，自然の動線軸を強調するように組み立てられている。これらの中庭は，変化に富んだ空間を提供するために，小道やテラス，プライベートの庭でさらに細分されている。北の中庭は，動線の道をつくりだすために，大地を切り分ける，並木に縁取られた小川のメタファーを使っている。この道は南の中庭へと入って行きながら，周囲に座る場所があり，緑地帯に向けて傾斜した草の床のある劇場の形をした空間を見せるように分岐して行く。

住戸ユニットのプランは，敷地のアメニティや太陽の方位に対する位置に従ってさまざまある。三つの基本的なストラテジーから平面計画の変化が生まれている。東西軸に沿ったリニアなユニットの，リビング，ダイニング，キッチンは南面して，太陽や緑地帯の眺めをほしいままにする。南北軸に沿ったリニアなユニットのリビング，ダイニング，キッチンは建物の長さに対し直角に向いている。これによって，リビング・ゾーンからは，朝と午後の光を受ける一方で中庭への眺めも得られる。中庭とリニアな集合住宅は，"オブジェ"の役割をする建物によってアクセントがつけられている。この建物は自動車の入口，主要な歩行者用の道と対応する焦点としての位置を占め，緑地帯に向いている。

建物は，クライアント（半官半民の設計開発会社）のつかう在来のメーソンリー工法と材料に従っている。建物の美的側面はエントリー，階段，ペントハウス，バルコニーを強調した建物の形態から生まれている。これらの形態は，亜鉛パネルでアクセントがつけられ，大胆な色のプラスターが主要な仕上げ材料である。

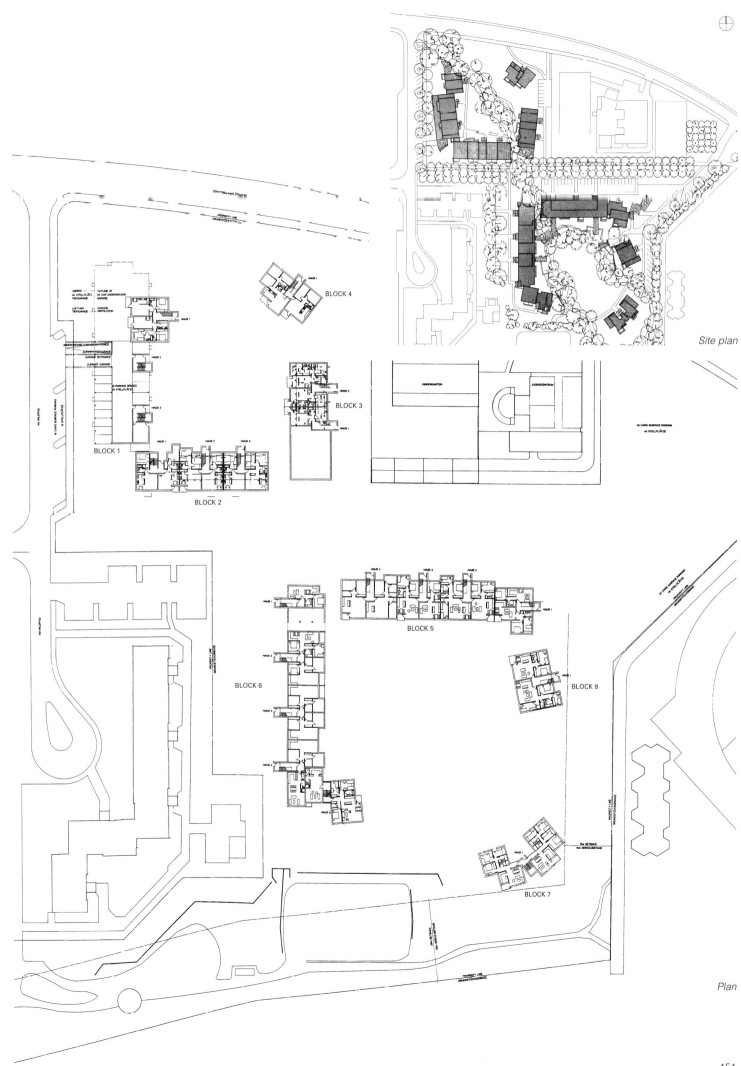

Site plan

Plan

Block 6　ブロック6

Block 7　ブロック7

Block 5 ブロック5

Block 5: north elevation

Block 5: south elevation

Block 5: view from court ブロック5：中庭より見る

Block 5: bicycle parking at east end ブロック5：東端の自転車置き場

1992–96
STEVEN HOLL

MAKUHARI BAY NEW TOWN
Chiba, Japan

View from east. South court house on center (red building)　東より見る。正面はサウス・コート・ハウス（赤い棟）

View from south gate　サウス・ゲートより見る

View from northwest. North gate house on roof level　北西より見る。屋上にはノース・ゲート・ハウス

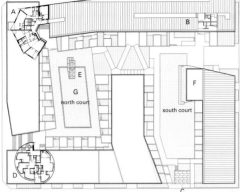
Roof

A East Gate House   E North Court House
B South Gate House F South Court House
C West Gate House   G Reflecting Pool
D North Gate House

Third floor

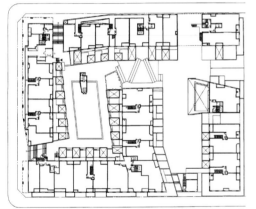
Second floor

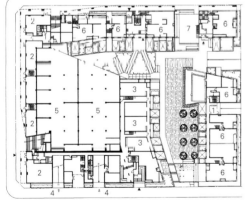

1 ENTRANCE/LOBBY
2 SHOP
3 BICYCLE PARKING
4 ENTRY TO CAR PARKING
5 UPPER PART OF CAR PARKING
6 HOUSING
7 POND

First floor S=1:1600

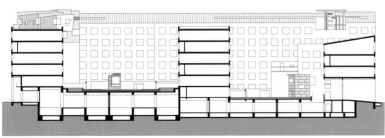
Longitudinal section S=1:1000

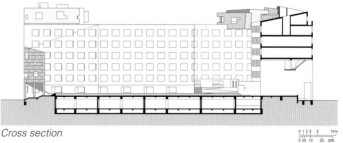
Cross section

North court with reflecting pool 水庭のあるノース・コート

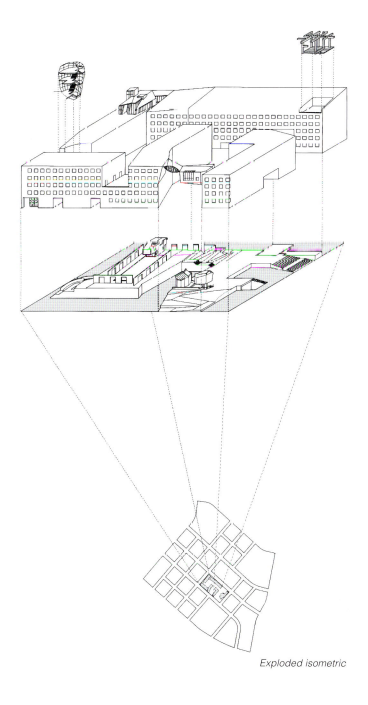

Exploded isometric

Lightweight = Activists = Sounds
Heavyweight = Bracketing Blocks = Silence

The new town of Makuhari is sited on dredged fill at the rim of Tokyo Bay. The urban planners have set rules for building height limits, tree-lined streets, areas for shops, etc. Each city block is to be designed by 3 or 4 different architects in an effort to achieve variety.

Our concept proposes the interrelation of two distinct types: silent heavyweight buildings and active lightweight structures.

The silent buildings shape the forms of urban space and passage with apartments entered via the inner garden courts. The concrete bearing wall structures have thick facades and a rhythmic repetition of openings (with variation in window or deck.) Slightly inflected, according to sunlight rules they gently bend space and passage, interrelating with movement and the lightweight structures.

Celebration of the miniature and natural phenomena are taken up in the lightweight activist force of individual characters and programs. These individuated "sounds" invade the heavyweight "silence" of the bracketing buildings.

Inspired by Basho's The Narrow Road to the Deep North, the semi-public inner gardens and the perspectival arrangement of activist houses form an inner journey.

While the interiors of apartments in the silent buildings are designed by Koichi Sone and Toshio Enomoto (Kajima Design), the activist structures by Steven Holl include:

1. East Gate House
   Sunlight Reflecting House
2. North Gate House
   Color Reflecting House
3. North Court House
   Water Reflecting House
4. South Court House
   Public meeting room
   House of Blue Shadow
5. West Gate House
   House of Fallen Persimmon
6. South Gate House
   Public Observation Deck
   House of Nothing

North Court House

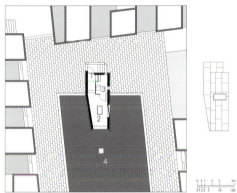

1 ENTRANCE
2 TEA ROOM
3 KITCHEN
4 REFLECTING POOL

First floor/roof S=1:500

View toward reflecting pool from inside　中から水庭を見る

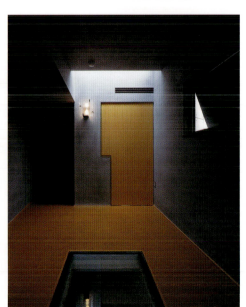

Interior　内部

South court and South court house　サウス・コートとサウス・コート・ハウス

South Court House

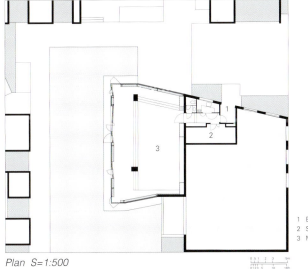
Plan S=1:500

1 ENTRANCE
2 STORAGE
3 MEETING ROOM

Meeting room　集会室

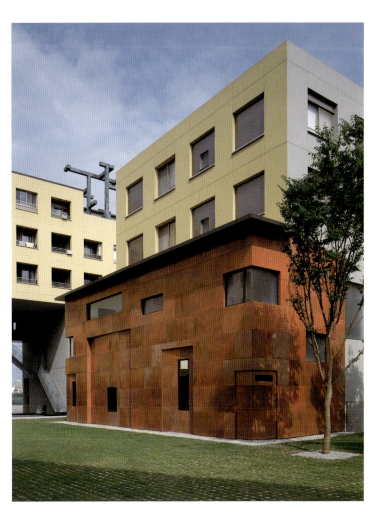

East gate house (on roof level) and North court house (below)
イースト・ゲート・ハウス（屋上）とノース・コート・ハウス（下）

East Gate House

Interior 内部 △▽

Interior 内部

View from roof 屋上より見る

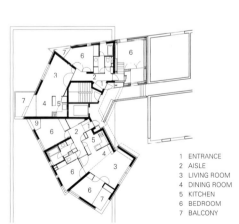

Plan S=1:500

1 ENTRANCE
2 AISLE
3 LIVING ROOM
4 DINING ROOM
5 KITCHEN
6 BEDROOM
7 BALCONY

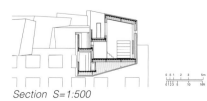

Section S=1:500

〈ライトウェイト＝アクティビスト＝サウンド〉
〈ヘビーウェイト＝ブラケット・ブロック＝静寂〉

幕張ニュータウンがあるのは東京湾岸の埋め立て地である。都市計画では建築の高さ制限，並木道，商業地域を定めることといったルールが定められていた。多様性を獲得することを目的として，3，4人の別々の建築家によって各々の街区は設計された。

この構想は異なる2種類の空間，すなわち静寂のヘビーウェイトの建築と，活気あるライトウェイトの構造の相互関係性に対する提案である。

サイレント・ビルディングを形成するのは都市空間とパッサージュ，内部の庭園からアクセスすることのできる集合住宅である。コンクリートの耐力壁のファサードは厚く，（窓やデッキといった，様々な）開口部がリズミカルに反復している。太陽光の動きに従いわずかに屈折した壁面は，緩やかに空間とパッサージュを折り曲げるようにして，リズミカルなライトウェイト構造へと結びついている。

細緻さと自然現象に対する祝福は，個々の空間の性格やプログラムが持つ軽やかで活動的な力として結実する。個々に峻別された「サウンド」は一括りの建築の持つ重厚な「静寂」の中へと侵入する。

松尾芭蕉の『奥の細道』は着想の源である。セミパブリックである内部の庭園と躍動する住宅の透視図法的空間構成が，内なる旅を生み出している。

サイレント・ビルディングのインテリアは曽根幸一氏と榎本敏男氏（鹿島建設）によるもので，スティーヴン・ホールによるアクティビスト・ストラクチュアは以下の住戸を含む：
1. イースト・ゲート・ハウス ─ 陽光を映す家
2. ノース・ゲート・ハウス ─ 色を映す家
3. ノース・コート・ハウス ─ 水を映す家
4. サウス・コート・ハウス ─ 集会室，青影の家
5. ウエスト・ゲート・ハウス ─ 落柿の家
6. サウス・ゲート・ハウス ─ 展望デッキ，無空の家

South Gate House

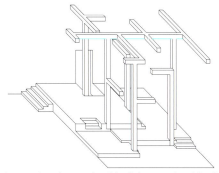

Isometric: observation "deck-house of nothing"

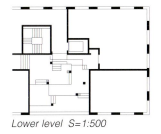

Lower level S=1:500

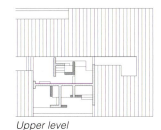

Upper level

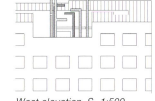

West elevation S=1:500

Interior 内部

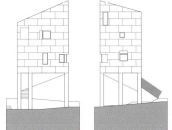

Elevations S=1:500

Sections

1 ENTRANCE
2 LIVING/DINING ROOM
3 KITCHEN

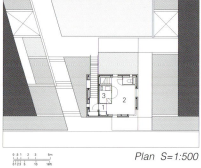

Plan S=1:500

West Gate House

North Gate House

View from roof 屋上より見る

North gate house ノース・ゲート・ハウス

Interior 内部

1 ENTRANCE
2 AISLE
3 LIVING ROOM
4 DINING ROOM
5 KITCHEN
6 BEDROOM
7 BATHROOM
8 WC
9 BALCONY

Plan S=1:500

Section S=1:500

1994–97
FRANCIS SOLER

SUITE SANS FIN
Rue Emile Durkheim, Paris, France

Francis Soler won in 1993 the competition for a 94 apartments building in front of the new National French Library, part of the "Seine Rive Gauche" urban development, with a project of living fresco.

I was greatly inspired by the frescos painted by Giulio Romano at the Palazzo del Té in Mantova while working on a series of images printed across long, horizontal bands of glass whose colors reverberate in gleaming daylight or under artificial lighting.

My first setting consisted of a succession of platforms piled one on top of the other. The concrete floor plates (80-meter long and 14-meter deep), facade columns and discontinued "curtain" stretched along the longitudinal axis in the building, created a completely free space on each level.

Then everybody could complete the interior to his wishes. Comparable to the fragmented and reassembled faces of Roman Cieslewicz, the backdrop of this fresco spread out across the glass and lend a certain intimacy to the inhabited spaces.

The wood of the joinery coexists in complete harmony with the colorless resin of the floor softening out the reddish tones of the colored cement. The thick Jatoba woodboards run along the narrow, Parisian balconies. The stainless steel handrails spin around the entire facade as if everything had been tied up. Two sets of blinds complete the facade: the one placed on the rim of the balconies assures summer comfort, and the other, between the outer and inner frames, guarantees intimacy at night.

From a thermal point of view, the building greatly profits from its compact proportions and from a third layer supporting the enameled images added to the transparent double glazing. Cold winter air heats up between the outer aluminum frame and the inner wooden frame. This complex also reduces noise nuisances by 42 db.

This is not anymore a matter of building in the traditional sense, but of territorial work, projecting a multitude of moving images onto reality. We are witnessing the importance of certain abstract forms (of the most ephemeral kind) as part of the construction of our cities today.
Francis Soler

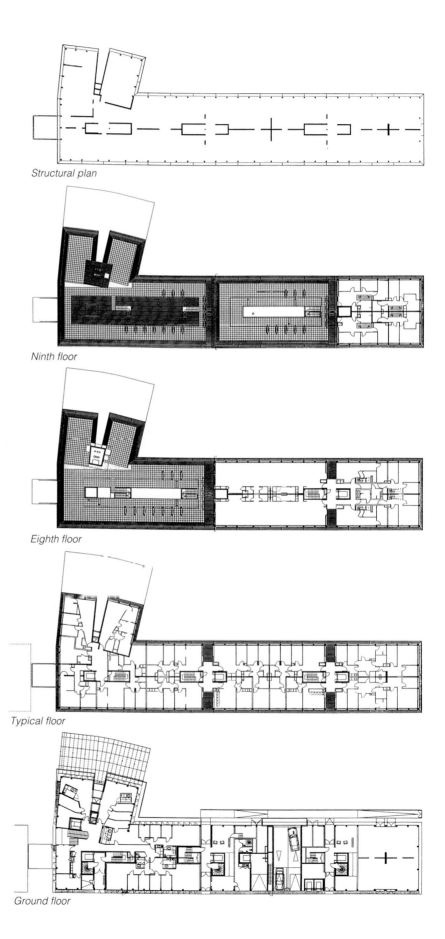

Structural plan

Ninth floor

Eighth floor

Typical floor

Ground floor

Overall view from street　道路側全景

1993年に行われたコンペの結果建設されたものである。セーヌ左岸の都市開発計画の一部である新国立図書館の向かいに位置する94戸からなるハウジングで，現代版フレスコ画がプリントされている。

昼間のぼんやりした光や人工照明の下で色彩が反響する長く水平に延びるガラス面にプリントすることになる絵を制作している間ずっと，マントヴァのパラッツォ・デル・テに描かれているジュリオ・ロマーノのフレスコ画に強く惹かれていた。

私の第1の設定は，上へ上へと積み重ねたプラットフォームの連なりで構成されている。コンクリートの床版（長さ80メートル，厚さ14メートル），ファサードに並ぶ列柱，断続する〈間壁〉が建物の長手軸に沿って延び，各階に完全な自由空間をつくりあげる。

つまり，各住人は好きなようにインテリアを完成できる。ローマン・シエスレヴィッチ（ポーランド出身のグラフィック・デザイナー。パリで活躍）の断片化し，再構成するグラフィック・デザインに比肩されるこのフレスコ画は，ガラス面を横断して広がり，住空間にある種の親密さを与えている。

床に塗られた無色のレジンと完璧な調和を見せている木製の建具類が色付きセメントの赤みを帯びた色調を和らげる。ジャトバの木からつくられた厚板が，幅の狭いパリ風のバルコニーに沿って張り渡され，ステンレス・スティール製の手摺がすべてを束ね上げるかのようにファサード全体に巡らされている。2対のブラインドがファサードを完結する。一つは，バルコニーの端に取り付けられ，夏の心地良さを保証し，もう一枚は，外枠と内枠の間に取り付けられて，夜のくつろぎをもたらす。

室内の温度の点からいうと，この建物はそのコンパクトな容積と，透明な2重ガラスに加え，エナメルで描かれた絵によって3層構成の恩恵を受けている。冬の冷たい空気は，アルミの外枠と木製の内枠の間で暖められる。これはまた，騒音を42デシベルにおさえる効果もあげている。

この建物はもはや，伝統的な意味での建物ではなく，おびただしい動的なイメージを現実の上に投影する，一地域的な作品である。私たちは，今日の都市を構築する一部として，（非常にはかない）ある抽象的な形態の重要性を提言しているのである。

（フランシス・ソレール）

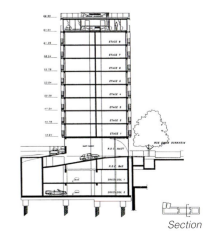

Section

Interior of apartment　住戸内部

View toward National library through illustration-printed window　イラストがプリントされた窓越しに国立図書館を見る

Illustration-printed window イラストがプリントされた窓

Roof terrace on ninth floor 10階ルーフ・テラス

1994–98
FREDERIC BOREL

HOUSING BUILDING RUE PELLEPORT
Paris, France

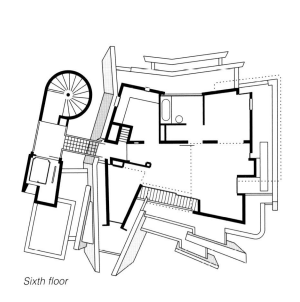
Sixth floor

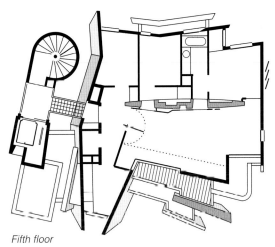
Fifth floor

Third floor

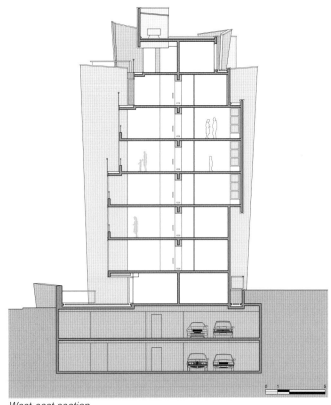
West-east section

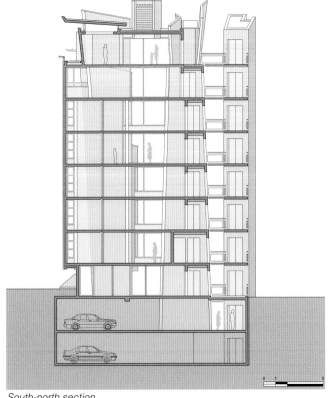
South-north section

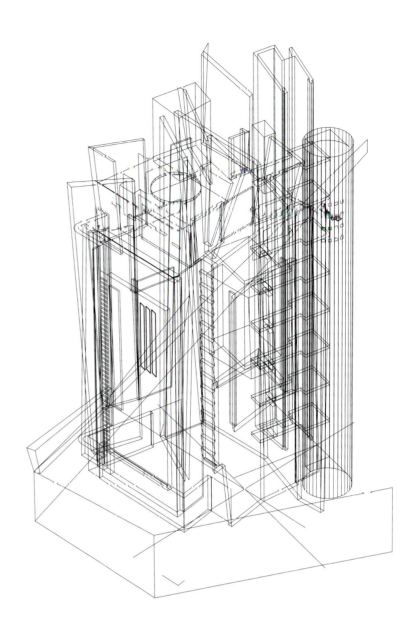

Recomposition of the Figure

This small housing project is situated in a strangely heterogenic neighborhood, due as much to its relief, very eventful allowing surprising views over Paris, as to its constructions. Inscribed on a triangular crossroad lot it relates the disemboweled rue des Pavillons where derisory relics of old Ménilmontant subsist and the rue Pelleport composed as a homogeneous closed corridor by its five to six story buildings. The site is finally blocked on the west by an autistic 17 story bar left behind since the constructive effervescence of the seventies.

The building does not borrow from any particular element of the context but poses as a liaison agent re-tying their impossible dialogue. The fragments forms, reflect the cut out shape of the old town maisonnettes; the angle is punctuated by an event marking the crossroads in the manner of a Borrominian scenography; the verticality is signified to introduce the real and brutal height of the concrete mass rising in the background. The housing blocks, the stair towers and the elevator are compressed one against the other, and in the same movement, the autonomous walls detach themselves producing an effect of depth and transparency, calming this universe of voids and plains very frankly opposed.

Taking the anatomy of the flower with its heart and corolla the first phase housing is organized around an opaque node which encloses cupboard and bathroom while at the periphery the petal fragments of wall enfold to divide the space of each level. Following this organic logic the interiors "naturally" orient themselves by the angle of their loggias (transformable to Jardins d'hiver) towards the sun and the view. Set back, and more associated with the natural elements, the second phase housing, frame through their opalescent cloud facade the forever renewed impression of the Parisian light on the urban landscape.

As in certain Giorgio de Chirico paintings (like the "great Metaphysician" composed with set squares) a folding effect is rendered by the juxtaposition and the superposition of fragments of plans. If the deconstruction of volumes as operated by neoplasticism is found here, the composition attaches itself, by means of the agglomeration of triangular surfaces, recomposing an enigmatic attentive figure, like an improbable look out, on the Parisian suburbs.
Richard Scoffier

形態の再構成

この小さなハウジング・プロジェクトは，奇妙に混成的な近隣のなかにあり，レリーフ状の非常に多彩な部分からなる建物のゆえに，パリに思いがけない眺めをもたらしている。十字路に面した三角形の敷地に刻み込まれた建物は，メニルモンタン地区の取るに足りない遺物のあるパヴィヨン通りと，5，6層の建物によって混成的な閉じられた回廊を構成しているペルポール通りに挟まれ，70年代の建設に対する熱狂によって残された自閉症的な17階建ての建物に西側を遮られている。

建物はこのコンテクストのなかからいかなる固有のエレメントも借用してきていないが，それらの間の不可能な対話を修復するコミュニケーション・エージェントとしての姿勢をとっている。古い街のメゾネットを切り抜いた形を反映させた断片的形態；ボロミーニ風の遠近画法のなかに交差点をマーキングすることで風穴の開けられた一画；コンクリート・マッスが背景のなかに立ち上がって，現実的で粗暴な高さを標榜することで表明する垂直性。ハウジング・ブロック，階段タワー，エレベータは周囲に逆らうように圧縮されている。そしてその同じ動きのなかに，自律する壁が自ら分離し，深度と透明性をつくりだし，このヴォイドと平面からなる宇宙が対立していることを率直に主張する。

花弁と芯からなる花の構成を応用している第1期のハウジングは，戸棚と浴室を囲む不透明な核の周りに配置され，一方，周辺部は花弁のような壁が各階のスペースを分割するように折り込まれる。この有機的なロジックに従って，内部はロジア（ウィンター・ガーデンへも転換可能）の角度によって「自然に」陽光と眺望に開かれる。セットバックし，自然の要素により親和性の高い第2期のハウジングは，乳白光を放つ曇ったファサードを通して，都市風景が常に更新されていく，パリらしい光の印象を枠取る。

いくつかのジョルジオ・デ・キリコの絵（三角定規で構成された『偉大なる形而上学者』のような）のように，折り込みは，プランの断片の並置，重ね合わせによって表現されている。もし，新造形主義による操作としてヴォリュームの脱構築がここに見られるとすれば，三角形の表面の無秩序な集合という方法によって建物に付加されている構成，パリ郊外のありそうにもない眺望のように，再構成された謎めいた形象がそれである。

（R・スコフィエ）

View from northwest 北西より見る

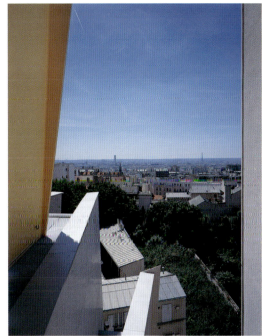
View of Paris from 7th floor　8階より見るパリの街

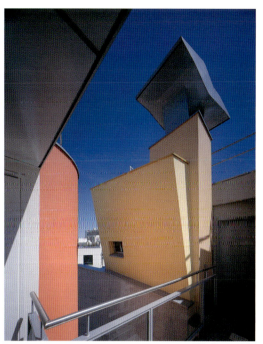
7th floor　8階

Entrance　玄関

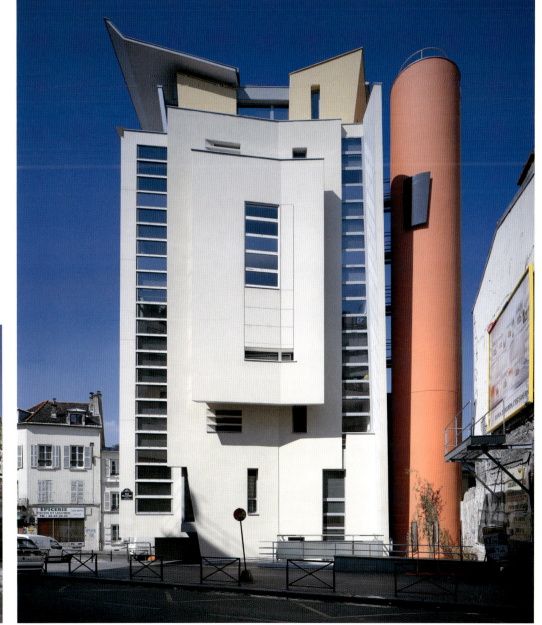
East elevation　東面

1994–2000
ARATA ISOZAKI (coordinator)
KAZUYO SEJIMA + AKIKO TAKAHASHI + CHRISTIAN HOLY + ELIZABETH DILLER

HIGHTOWN KITAGATA
Kitagata, Gifu, Japan

Overall view from southwest: Takahashi wing (left), Holy wing (center) and Sejima wing (right)　南西側全景：高橋棟（左），ホーリィ棟（中央），妹島棟（右）

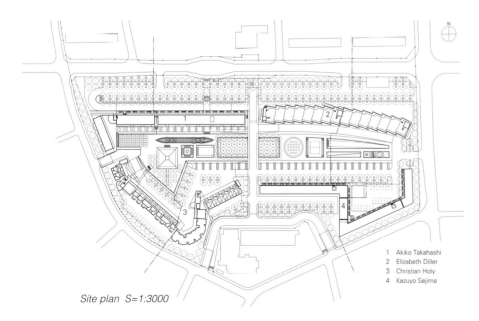

Site plan S=1:3000

1 Akiko Takahashi
2 Elizabeth Diller
3 Christian Holy
4 Kazuyo Sejima

Public social housing in Japan, which were first administered in the years following World War II, is said to have become quite obstinate and rigid. Of course in reality, various efforts have been made. Just before the beginning of the 21st century, coordinator Arata Isozaki proposed an urban social housing model as a kind of general solution. It was a kind of work that followed the intensity of Nexus World, a 1991 project in Fukuoka that challenged the notion of commercially developed condominiums.

A team of four architects, one landscape architect (Martha Schwartz), one designer (Emi Fukuzawa), and one artist (Aiko Miyawaki) were gathered from both within and outside of Japan, all of whom were female. The project first began with proposals for plan types in the residential building. According to Isozaki's words, this resulted in a group of urban-scaled residential buildings that were untouched by "masculine nature" (although one could also

argue that it was an act of taming such nature by a group of women led by a male coordinator).

In actuality, the project involves a 35,000 square meter block of existing public housing, with slab-like buildings of 30 meters height that were built along a warped landscape surrounding a large courtyard. Each of the plan types, which were designed to question the inflexibility of modern apartment complexes, proposed open plans that were broken up into horizontal and vertical sections with duplexes and movable partitions. This was a revaluation of the ideal type, a call for freedom from apartment planning that have become increasingly subdivided and compartmentalized. Of these, the building designed by Sejima was especially distinct, where its exterior directly showed off the chains of wall-separated rooms that were connected through a sun porch/engawa, creating an appearance of a thickly layered mass.

第2次世界大戦後に整備された日本の公的ソーシャル・ハウジングの仕組みは非常に硬直化していると言われている。もちろん，現実には多様な実践が行われているが，21世紀を直前にしたこの段階で総合コーディネーター・磯崎新は，一般解としての都市型ソーシャルハウジングのモデルを提起しようとした。1991年に福岡で，デベロッパーによる分譲型集合住宅に対する揺さぶりをかけた「ネクサスワールド」に連続する取り組みとも言える。

まず，国内外から4人の建築家，1人のランドスケープ・アーキテクト（マーサ・シュワルツ），1人のデザイナー（福澤エミ），1人のアーティスト（宮脇愛子）が指名された。全て女性である。そして設計開始にあたり，住戸棟の平面型に対する提案を出発点とする。かくして磯崎の言によれば，「男性原理」に貫通されていない，アーバンスケールの住居棟群が生まれた（ただし，男性コーディネーターに導かれた女性たちによる，原理を飼い慣らした実践とも言えよう）。

具体的には，既存の県営住宅団地のワンブロック35,000平米の敷地に対し，4人による高さ30メートル弱の板状の建物が，変形した土地形状に沿って大きな中庭を構成するように取り囲む。近代的な集合住宅計画に対する提案となった各平面型は，オープンプランをメゾネットや可動間仕切で水平垂直に分節するもので，より個室化・細分化の進んだ住戸プランの状況に対する，自由を求めた理念型の再評価とも言える。その中で，壁体で仕切られた居室を連続させ，「広縁」でつなぎ合わせたプランを立面に表出させ，重層した解像度をつくり出した「妹島棟」は，異質であった。

Looking west: courtyard surrounded by 4 wings　西を見る：4棟に囲まれた中庭

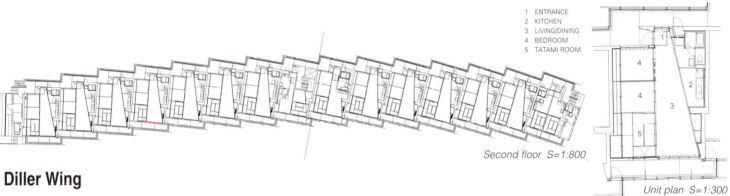

Diller Wing

Second floor　S=1:800

1　ENTRANCE
2　KITCHEN
3　LIVING/DINING
4　BEDROOM
5　TATAMI ROOM

Unit plan　S=1:300

Overall view from southwest　南西側全景

Corridor on north　北側廊下

Overall view from southwest 南西側全景

Sejima Wing

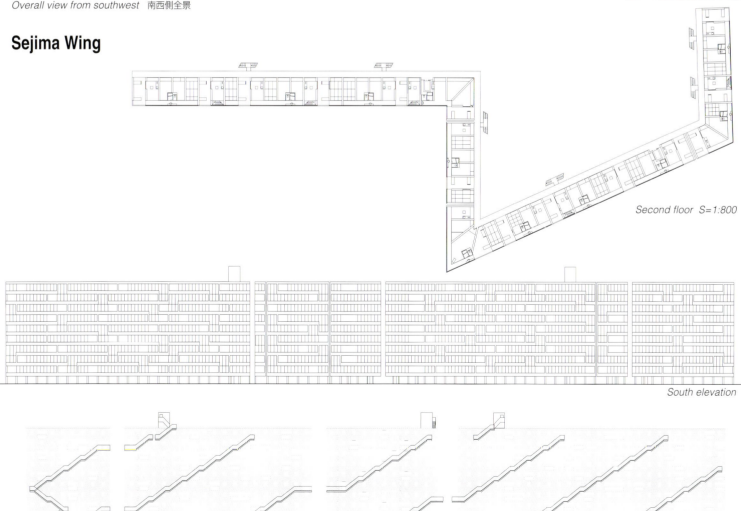

Second floor S=1:800

South elevation

North elevation S=1:1000

South elevation 南面

Sejima Wing

1 TERRACE
2 BEDROOM
3 DINING/KITCHEN
4 TATAMI ROOM
5 VOID
6 STORAGE
7 SUN PORCH

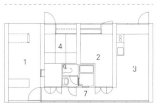 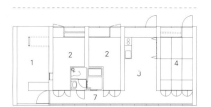 

Unit plans S=1:300

Dining/kitchen: terrace on left　食堂／台所：左はテラス

Sun porch　縁側

North elevation　北面

Section (common corridor)

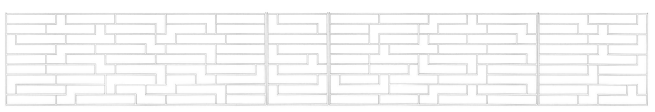

Section (sun porch)

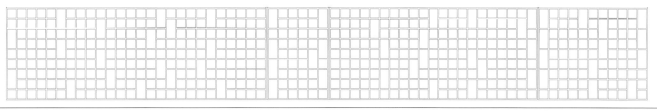

Section (unit)　S=1:1000

View from southeast　南東より見る

Pilotis　ピロティ

Interior of unit B　住戸B内部

Interior of unit A　住戸A内部

Takahashi Wing

3rd - 6th floor　S=1:800

Unit A　S=1:300

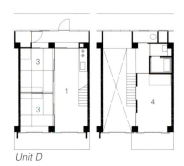

Unit B　　　　Unit D

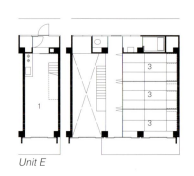

Unit E

1　DINING/KITCHEN
2　COURT
3　TATAMI ROOM
4　ROOM

Holy Wing

Second floor S=1:800

Triplex: living/dining トリプレックス：居間／食堂

Overall view from south 南側全景

Triplex: hall トリプレックス：ホール

Section S=1:500

1 ROOM
2 TATAMI ROOM
3 BALCONY
4 ENTRANCE
5 HALL
6 KITCHEN
7 LIVING/DINING
8 STUDIO

Triplex type: lower level S=1:300

Middle level

Upper level

Duplex type: lower level

Upper level

1995–98
KAZUHIRO KOJIMA + KAZUKO AKAMATSU / CAT

SPACE BLOCK KAMISHINJO
Osaka, Japan

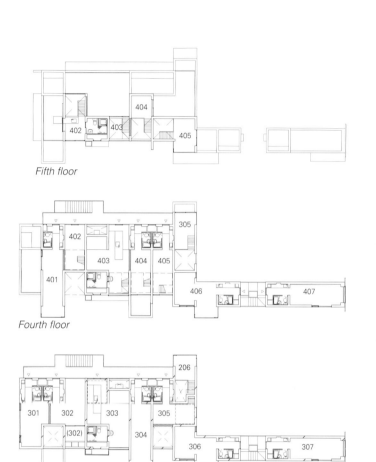
Fifth floor
Fourth floor
Third floor

Second floor

1 SHOP
2 STORAGE FOR RENT
3 OFFICE

First floor S=1:400

Overall view from east 東側全景

An apartment designed by using Basic Space Block (hereinafter referred to as BSB) was completed. BSB was devised as a tool to think about design in a different method from starting by drawing a plan. It is a model to capture space as a toy building block with more than 3 connected cubes. There are 2 types, liner and L-shaped, with 3 cubes, and 5 kinds, with different placement of the bottom surface on the ground. There are 8 types with 4 cubes and 29 types with 5 cubes. The reason for basing cube is 'ease of piling up' and it is free to model parts by stretching or tilting after they are stacked.

House-NS was the smallest model of combined 2 BSBs, which was named Cube Type L made of 4 parts. This time 22 BSBs were used for the second floor and above. To build a gigantic model such as restructured Kowloon Walled City is possible to plot, if several hundreds of BSBs are combined. Quality of parts is guaranteed even with a large group with this method, because each block that becomes a unit is space furnished with characteristic 'shape'.

Now about Kamishinjo, it is an urban apartment, which was realized after a long time for us. In previous projects such as SA-House, we tried to generate a singular point by capturing architecture as a part or a fragment of city and by a way to gather elements and raising its density. It was a direction to concentrate the surrounding environment inside the site. In the project, the use of BSB turns the vector around and takes in extensibility to city. On the other hand, the idea of parts (residential unit) to be advantageous over the entire architecture is the same, so both lets the boundary of architecture to dissolve into the surroundings.

One BSB is one unit in Kamishinjo. If a rule is to make a unit with 2 BSBs, 2-room apartment that looks like piling up House-NS is created. Such a residence that is connected from the second floor to the fifth floor within the building is possible. I would like to design jointly with logic of 'Black/White', if there is a chance.

Here, each side of cube is 2.4 meter (inside measurement is 2.18 meter, only story height is 2.5 meter). It required courage to decide the dimension up to this point. We studied in full scale many times. Making the side a little larger makes the designer feel at ease. However, it would enlarge the volume of each unit and would reduce the number of cubes that compose BSB, so it would be inconvenient. The completed space has no tight feeling, owing to the effect of a bend in the building, neutral and white only finish and a BSB with maximum extent opening.

Although wall type reinforced concrete was chosen for structure, upper and lower walls did not align. So the wall arrangement was three-dimensionally analyzed. This led to a challenge to a new possibility for a wall type reinforced concrete structure. The completed building shows a different appearance from a building that was built by just making an opening on a box.
Kazuhiro Kojima

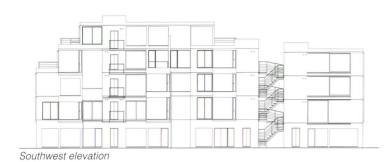
Southwest elevation

Southeast elevation

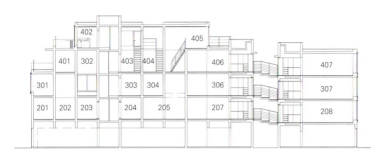

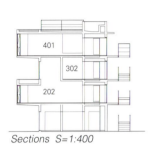

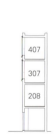

Sections S=1:400

Southeast elevation　南東面

View from northwest　北西より見る

Room 404

Room 205

Room 303

　ベーシック・スペース・ブロック（以下BSB）を使って設計したアパートメントが完成した。BSBは平面図を描くことから始めるのとは異なった方法で設計を思考するツールとして考えたものだ。立方体3個以上をつなぎあわせた積み木として空間をとらえるモデルである。立方体3個だと一直線かL型の2タイプでどの面を下にするかで見ると5種類となる。4個つないだものだと8タイプ、5個で29タイプある。立方体を基準にした理由は「積み易さ」であり、積んだ後で一部を引き延ばしたり傾けたりとモデリングするのは自由だ。

　「那須の別荘」は立体L型と名付けた4個繋ぎのBSB2個の組み合わせによる最小モデルだった。今回は2階以上の部分で22個のBSBを用いている。何百ものBSBを組み合わせれば九龍城砦を再構成したような巨大なモデルも構想可能である。単位となる個々のブロック自体が特性ある「かたち」を持ったスペースだから、この方法では大きな群でも部分の質は保証される。

　さて「上新庄」だが、これは私たちにとって久しぶりに実現した都市型アパートメントである。以前の「桜台アパートメント」などでは都市の部分、あるいは断片として建築をとらえて、要素の集まり方とその密度を上げることで特異点を発生させようとしていた。それは周囲の環境を敷地の中に凝集する方向であった。ここではBSBを用いることでベクトルが逆となり都市への拡張性を持つ。一方で部分（住戸）が建築全体に対して優位に立つ発想は同じだから、どちらも建築の輪郭が周囲へ溶け込んでいく。

　「上新庄」ではBSB1個が1住戸である。もしBSB2個で1住戸というルールにすれば、「那須」を積み上げたような2ルーム・アパートができあがる。建築の中で2階から5階まで繋がる住戸なども可能だ。機会があったら「黒／白」のロジックと併せて設計してみたい。

　立方体の一辺はここでは2.4メートル（内法2.18メートル、階高のみ2.5メートル）である。ここまで寸法を詰めるには勇気がいる。何度も原寸で検討した。一辺をもう少し大きくする方が設計者としては安心だが、それでは戸当たりヴォリュームが大きくBSBをつくる立方体数を減らすことになるからうまみがない。完成したスペースは折れ曲がりがあること、ニュートラルな白1色の仕上げ、空間断面いっぱいの開口BSBなどの効果で窮屈さは感じない。

　RC壁式構造を採用したが、上下に壁が通らないため壁配置を立方体に解析しており、それが壁式の新しい可能性への挑戦となった。実現した建築はボックスに開口をあけるのとは異なる現れ方をしている。

（小嶋一浩）

1999–2004
KENGO KUMA

SHINONOME APARTMENT BUILDING
Tokyo, Japan

Site plan S=1:10000

A proposal for a new type of urban rented housing complex by a public entity (organization for promoting urban development).

New types of layout and unit plannings are made based on the idea that collective housing in the city would transform, from the family-type during the years of economic growth, to SOHO-type and hybrid function-type that suit more mature phases. In terms of layout, with less focus on natural lighting from south, semi-outdoor spaces such as 'communication voids' are used in abundance to form a sort of stereoscopic streets. The latter are connected to each unit via a glass-covered opening. This is a revival of the schema of alleyway at human scales with residential units that open onto them, which once used to be the basis of urban spaces in Japan. Open, studio-type residential units proposed here to cater to flexible, SOHO-types of contemporary lifestyle, also proved to be haply analogous to the traditional residential plan (such as dirt floor and inner court) in Japan.

公的主体（都市機構）による，新しいタイプの都市型複合型賃貸集合住宅の提案。

都市の集合住宅は，高度成長期のファミリータイプから，成熟期に適応するSOHO型，複合機能型に変化するという基本的認識のもとに，新しい配置計画，ユニット計画を行った。配置においては南面採光を重視せず，コミュニケーションヴォイド等の半外部空間を多用した，1種の立体型街路を提案し，その立体型街路と，各ユニットの間は，ガラスの開口でつないだ。かつての日本の都市空間の基本であった，ヒューマンスケールの路地空間と，それに向かって開かれたオープンな住戸ユニットという考え方を再生した。住戸ユニットにおいては，SOHO型のフレキシブルなライフスタイルに適応するよう，オープンなワンルームを提案し，これもまた，結果として日本の伝統的住戸プラン（たとえば土間や通り庭）に，期せずして類似したものとなった。

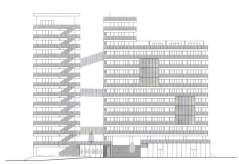
South elevation

North elevation

East elevation

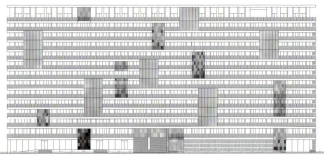
West elevation S=1:1200

Overall view from west: building on right is designed by Riken Yamamoto　西側全景：右の棟は山本理顕による設計

View from east　東より見る

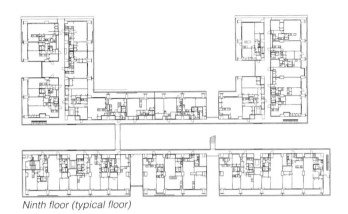
Ninth floor (typical floor)

Courtyard of entrance エントランスの中庭

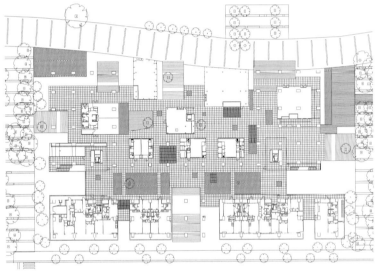
Second floor

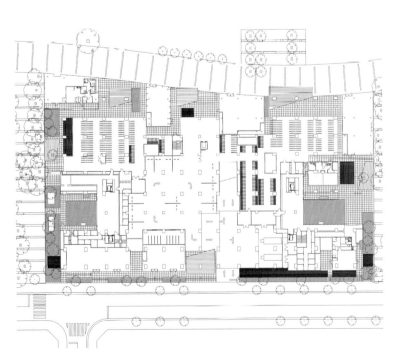
First floor S=1:1200

Bridges ブリッジ

View from deck on south 南側のデッキより見る

Entrance エントランス

1. RESIDENCE
2. SMALL OFFICE
3. SHOP
4. ROOF GARDEN
5. VOID
6. BRIDGE
7. ATRIUM
8. PARKING

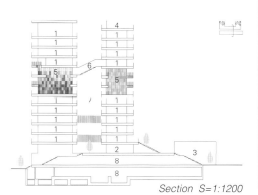
Section S=1:1200

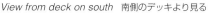
Communication void コミュニケーション・ヴォイド

Residence on fourteenth floor 14階の住居

Residence: maisonette type メゾネット・タイプの住居

187

1999–2004
NORMAN FOSTER

ALBION RIVERSIDE DEVELOPMENT
London, U.K.

The development of Albion Wharf reinforces a growing new community on the south bank of the Thames, alongside the Foster studio between Battersea and Albert bridges. A mixed-use development, its ingredients are designed to promote a lively urban quarter where people can live, work and enjoy life in the city.

The scheme comprises three separate buildings linked by new public spaces and routes. Shops, business spaces, cafés and leisure facilities are grouped at ground level, with parking below and residences, including low-cost housing, above.

The principal building on the waterfront is eleven storeys high. Its massing is designed to respect the heights of neighbouring buildings and to frame the view of the river from the opposite bank. The building arcs back from the river's edge in an asymmetrical crescent to create a public space alongside the river walk.

The facades are principally of glass, used in a range of translucency to create elevations which vary in appearance and sparkle according to prevailing light conditions and changing viewpoints. On the river facade, curved balconies with clear glass balustrades are accessed through full-height sliding glazed panels, which allow the apartments to open out onto the water. The strong horizontal line of the balconies reinforces a sense of visual order, allowing the clutter of inhabitation to proliferate but not dominate.

The southern facade is expressed as a veil of aluminium rods, which forms a rain-screen in front of a metal and glass weathering layer. The roof continues the building's curving form, appearing to wrap over and around in a single sweep.

Plaza on south 南側プラザ

Overall view from north: studio of Foster and Partners on left 北側全景：左はフォスター・アンド・パートナーズ事務所

Pilotis ピロティ

Entrance lobby エントランス・ロビー

Detail of north elevation 北側面のディテール

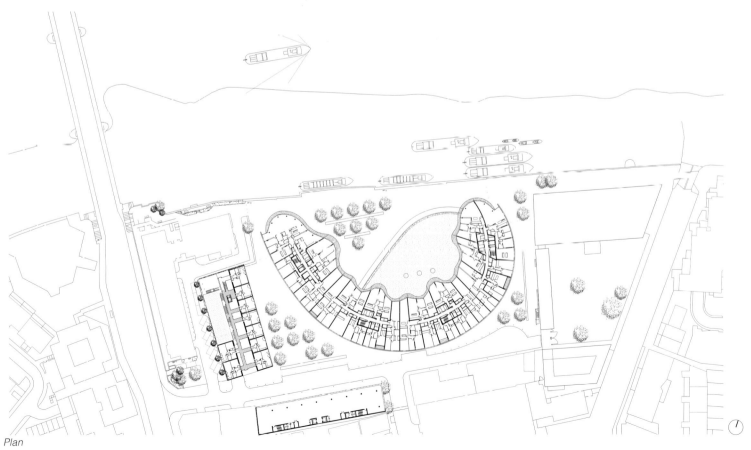

Plan

Entrance lobby エントランス・ロビー

Roof garden on first floor 2階庭園

Interior of apartment 住戸内部

アルビオン河岸の開発は，バターシーとアルバート・ブリッジの間，フォスターのスタジオに沿ったテムズ川のサウス・バンクに広がる目下成長中の新しいコミュニティにさらに勢いを与えるだろう。混合用途の開発で，それぞれの構成要素は，人々が生活し，仕事し，楽しめる活気のある都市域をつくるようなデザインとなっている。

建物は，新しい公共空間と通路でつながれた3棟構成である。店舗，ビジネス・スペース，カフェ，娯楽施設が1階にまとめられ，駐車場は地階，ローコスト・ハウジングを含めた住宅が上階を占める。

川に面した中心的な棟は，11階建。その外形は，周囲の建物の高さに配慮し，対岸からの川の眺めを枠取るようにデザインされている。建物の弧は，川縁から非対称の半月形を描いて後退し，川岸の遊歩道のそばに公共空間をつくりだす。

ファサードは主にガラスで構成され，様々なレベルの半透明な面を組み合わせることで，その時々の光の状態や見る位置により表情を変え輝きを変える立面をつくりだす。川に面しては，透明ガラスの手摺のついた湾曲するバルコニーが並び，天井まで届くガラスパネルの引戸によって，各住戸は水に向かって開かれる。バルコニーの水平に伸びる強いラインは，視覚的な秩序感を強め，大勢が住むことから生まれる入り乱れた表情の増殖を許しつつ行き過ぎないところで抑えている。

南面は，耐候性のあるメタルとガラスの外壁の前をアルミ・ロッドがベールのように覆い，雨よけのスクリーンを構成する。屋根は壁の曲線の延長上，1枚の曲面で包み込む。

2002–05
BIG/BJARKE INGELS

VM-HOUSES
Copenhagen, Denmark

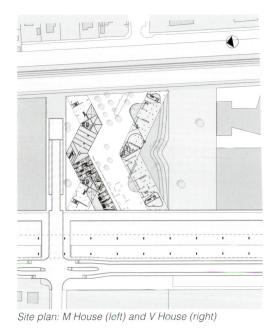

Site plan: M House (left) and V House (right)

V House Vハウス

From right to left, V House, M House and the Mountain (pp.230-235) 右からVハウス，Mハウス，ザ・マウンテン (pp.230-235)

M House: view from the Mountain on north Mハウス：北側のザ・マウンテンから見る

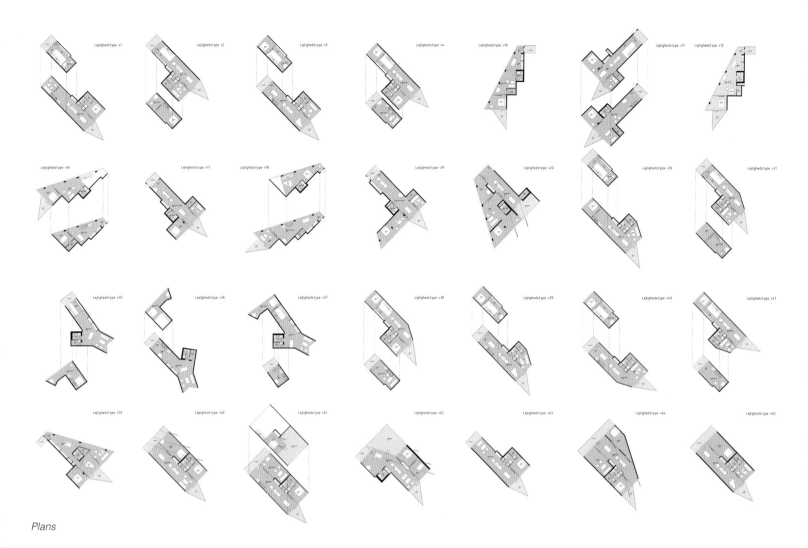

Plans

The VM Houses, shaped like a V and an M when seen from above, is the first residential project to be built in the new district of Copenhagen known as Ørestaden. The upcoming neighbourhood is connected to the center of the city by the new metro system.

The manipulated perimeter block of the V building is clearly defined in its four corners, but opened internally and along the sides. The vis-à-vis with the neighbouring M house is eliminated by pushing the slab in its centre, ensuring diagonal views to the vast, open fields around. The building volume provides optimal air, daylight and views to all apartments with triangular-shaped balconies characterizing the south facing facade. All apartments have a double-height space to the north and wide panoramic views to the south.

People can access the apartments from a central corridor that cuts through the building volume and opens up towards daylight and views at each end. The corridors create connections to elevators and staircases and function as a local community where people can meet spontaneously and children can play. The central hallway function as a public space, imitating random bullet holes penetrating the building.

A similar logic of the diagonal slab is used in the M building, although in this case it is broken down into smaller portions. Here, the typology of Le Corbusier's Unitè d'habitation is reinterpreted and mutated: the central corridors are short and receive light from both ends. Individual terraces are all on the south facing side of the building, and the roof terrace can be reached from the central corridors.

The apartments are characterized by the interaction of mutually complementing rooms—with double-height studios near kitchens and living rooms, with large and open rooms that can be broken down into smaller ones and spatial attics which are naturally lit.

The VM Houses are made up of simple but exquisite materials with large glass facades framed by fancy wood. Floors are made up of solid oak wood, and dark, hard wood have been used for the balcony floors. Walls and ceilings appear with a somewhat raw finish in white concrete, and all internal stairs and handrails come in white painted steel. All the apartments' external walls are made up of glass.

As the first residential complex in the area, it was important to create an inviting environment. To provide public space around the buildings, the V volume is raised on five metre high columns, opening up the courtyard to the park area on the south side while the facades are articulated with niches and angles, creating a series of informal meeting places.

One of the most important aspects of this housing scheme focuses on the development of diverse apartment typologies, ranging from single-floor plans to triplexes. The 114-unit V building is composed of 40 different apartment types, while the M building with its 95 units contains 40 typologies.

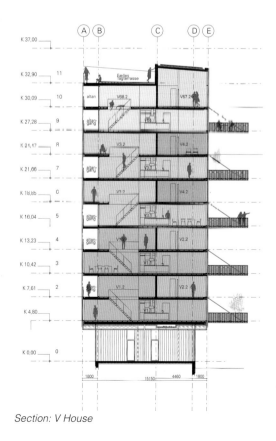

Section: V House

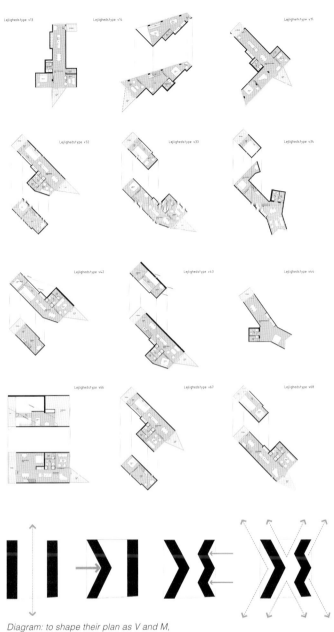

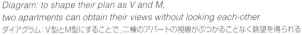

Diagram: to shape their plan as V and M,
two apartments can obtain their views without looking each-other
ダイアグラム：V型とM型にすることで，二棟のアパートの視線がぶつかることなく眺望を得られる

V House: facade detail　Vハウス：壁面ディテール

　上空から見るとVとMの形をしているVMハウスは，コペンハーゲンの新興開発地であるオレスタッデンにおいて，最初に計画された住宅コンプレックスである。この地域は近い将来，新たに整備される地下鉄によって中心地区と接続される予定である。

　無理なく構成されたV棟のペリメーター・ブロック（街区に沿って立つ建物）は，その四つの角部では完全に閉じられているが，その内側と側面では開放的である。中央のスラブを押込むことで，隣接するM棟と正面から向き合うことを避け，周囲の開けた土地に向かって抜ける，斜めの方向への視線を確保している。建物のヴォリュームは，ファサードを特徴づける三角形のバルコニーをもつ各住戸へ快適な風，日照，眺望を提供する。全住戸は，北側に2層分の空間を設けており，南側からは広範囲なパノラマが望める。各住戸へは建物の中央を貫く廊下からアクセスする。この廊下は，その両端から自然光と眺望を得られる。廊下は，エレベータや階段とのつながりを生み出し，住人同士が顔を合わせたり，子供が遊ぶことのできるローカル・コミュニティ形成の場として機能する。

　スラブを折り曲げるという同様の手法は，M棟でも用いられている。こちらでは，V棟よりも小さな部分へと分解している。ル・コルビュジエのユニテ・ダビタシオンを再考して変形を試みた―中央の廊下を短くし，その両端から採光する。住戸の個々のテラスはすべて南側に置かれており，ルーフ・テラスへは中央の廊下からアクセスできる。各住戸は，台所付近に高さ2層分のスタジオ，小部屋として間仕切り可能な広い空間，そして屋根裏部屋付きの居間など，相互補完的に部屋が連続している。

　これら二つの棟は，シンプルでありながら，美しいマテリアルと木のフレームによる巨大なガラス・ファサードで構成されている。床はオーク材，バルコニーの床は濃い色の堅い木材が用いられている。壁と天井はホワイト・コンクリート造で幾分荒々しい表情をもたせている。内部階段と手摺りは白く塗装したスティール製。全住戸の外壁はガラス製である。

　この一帯で，最初に計画される住宅コンプレックスとして，魅力ある環境をつくり出すことが必要不可欠であった。建物の廻りに公共のスペースを設けるため，V型平面のヴォリュームを高さ5メートルの柱でもち上げて，南側の公園に向かって中庭を開放した。その一方で，ファサードを分節するくぼみの部分や角部によってファサードを整え，親しみやすい交流の場をつくり出している。

　このコンプレックスにおいて最も重要なコンセプトは，住戸のタイポロジーの多様性であった。1層の住戸から3層にわたる住戸まで用意している。V棟は40タイプを含む114戸，M棟も40タイプを含む全95戸で構成されている。

V House (left) and M House (right)　Vハウス（左）とMハウス（右）

M House: main entrance　Mハウス：メイン・エントランス

M House: interior　Mハウス：内部

M House　Mハウス

M House: corridor　Mハウス：廊下

V House: main entrance　Vハウス：メイン・エントランス

2002–05
RYUE NISHIZAWA

MORIYAMA HOUSE
Tokyo, Japan

Evening view from east 東側夕景

A project consisting of a housing for extremely small studios for rent called 'one-room mansions' and an independent residence built on the same site. The vicinity is a residential area that preserves the good old atmosphere of downtown Tokyo, a charming urban block where double to triple-storied, mid-scaled apartments and houses stand at small intervals in orderly rows.

Assuming that to incorporate the owner's residence into the housing complex would make the volume much too large compared to the neighboring buildings, we chose to separate the houses and arrange them independently. Our idea was that by doing so this area's urban pattern made of repeated sequence of small buildings and voids might be maintained, and each household might be provided with a tiny garden. Because the group of independent buildings has no common structure as a whole, size and shape of each building can be designed separately. As a result a variety of house types came to be created: triple-storied house; square house half buried below ground; house with extremely high ceiling; house surrounded by a garden on four sides. They are crammed into the site, generating a diversity of exterior spaces such as small gardens and alleyways. Relationship between each house with its garden is different in variation. Our attempt is to create living spaces typical of Tokyo, where life is not enclosed solely within the indoor space but continues from indoors to garden and alleyways.

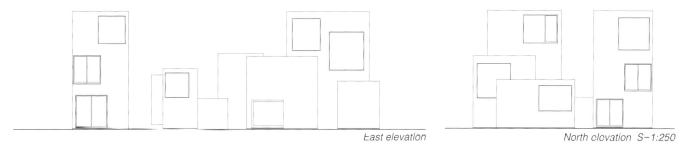

East elevation　　　*North elevation S=1:250*

View from north　北より見る

非常に小さな賃貸住戸が集まる，ワンルームマンションと呼ばれる集合住宅，それと専用住宅一つが，一つの敷地の中に建つ計画である。周辺は昔からの東京の下町の雰囲気を残す住宅地で，2，3階建ての中規模のアパートや住宅が，お互いに小さな間隔を空けて秩序だって並ぶ，魅力的な街区である。

要求されたオーナー住宅と賃貸集合住宅を一体としてつくると，ヴォリュームが周りの建物に比べて大変大きくなってしまうため，私たちは各住宅を離して，各々を独立配置することにした。そのことによって，建物と隙間が細かく反復してゆくこの地区の都市パターンを継承できるのではないかと思い，また，各住戸に小さな庭を与えることができるのではないかと考えた。独立して建つ建物群は，共通した全体構造を持たないため，各々別々に空間の大きさや形を決めることができる。そのため，3階建ての住宅，半地下の正方形の住宅，天井高が非常に高い住宅，庭に四周囲まれた住宅など，いろいろな住戸タイプが生まれた。それらはひしめき合うように敷地に並びながら，その間に小さな庭や路地のような，様々な屋外空間をつくり出している。各々の住宅は，庭との関係においてもいろいろなバリエーションを持っている。生活が屋内空間だけで閉ざされるのではなく，むしろ室内と庭・路地などに連続していくような，東京らしい住空間をつくり出そうと考えている。

Site plan S=1:2000

House B (left), house A (center) and house C (right, bathroom)　B棟(左)、A棟(中央)とC棟(右、浴室)

Third floor of house A (master bedroom)　A棟3階(主寝室)

Living room of house I　I棟、居間

Garden: house G (right) and house C (left, bathroom)　中庭：G棟（右）とC棟（左，浴室）

House I (right) and house G (left)　I棟（右）とG棟（左）

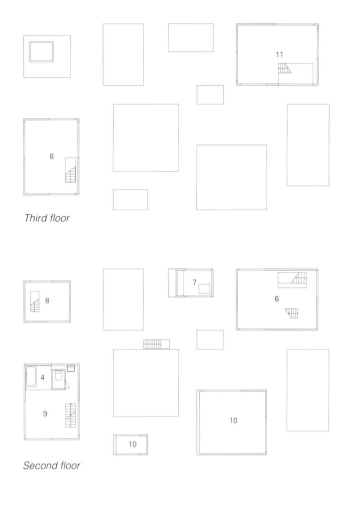

Third floor

Second floor

First floor

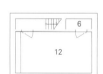

Basement S=1:250

1 LIVING ROOM
2 DINING ROOM/KITCHEN
3 ANNEX
4 BATHROOM
5 GARDEN
6 STORAGE
7 LIBRARY
8 BEDROOM
9 SUNROOM
10 VOID
11 MASTER BEDROOM
12 STUDIO
13 DRY AREA

Aperture of house F　F棟，開口部

Aperture and staircase of house F　F棟，開口部と階段

202

Glazed corridor between house G and house H (bathroom)
G棟とH棟（浴室）をつなぐガラスの廊下

View toward house C (bathroom) over house B (dining room/kitchen)　B棟（食堂／台所）越しにC棟（浴室）を見る

View of garden from house J　J棟から中庭を見る

▽ *Glazed corridor: view from house B (dining room/kitchen) toward house A (living room)*
ガラスの廊下：B棟（食堂／台所）からA棟（居間）を見る

Dining room/kitchen of house E　E棟，食堂／台所

2002–07
MORPHOSIS

MADRID SOCIAL HOUSING
Carabanchel, Madrid, Spain

Roofscape of wind towers　換気塔が並ぶ屋上

View from east 東より見る

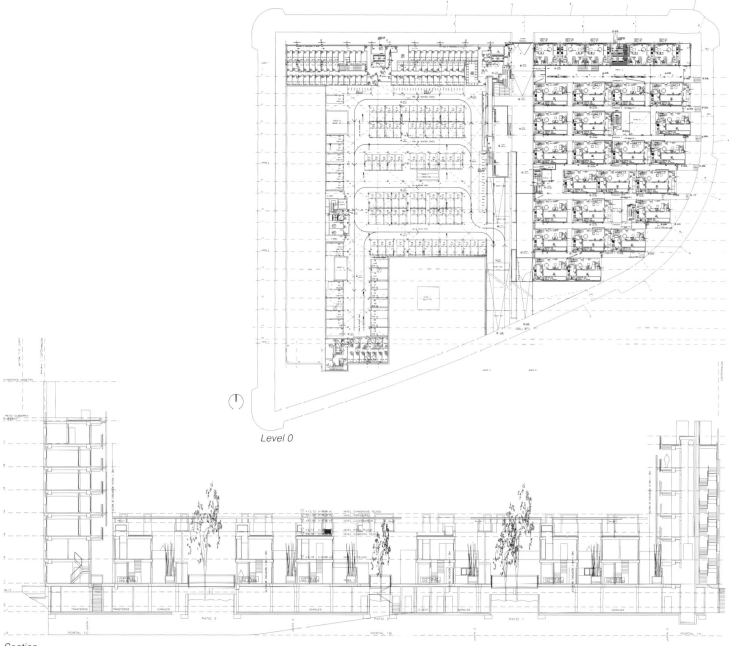
Level 0

Section

In a suburban Madrid neighborhood of conventional, anonymous housing blocks, we devised a typology of porosity to suit the social ideals of this project type. As an alternative to towering blocks of faceless units, this project explores a radically different social model that integrates landscape and village topologies. By grafting properties commonly found in detached villas onto this low-income housing project we achieved a multi-family living complex with amenities such as loggias, green spaces, and domestically scaled massing that are not normally found in public housing in Spain.

A layer of landscape overlaid upon a facade composed of a series of open spaces and idiosyncratic punctures combine to break down the institutional nature of the public housing project. The basic parti is an extruded "J": a low-rise "village" building, flanked by a tall, slender bar to the north and a lower multi-level bar building to the south. Open spaces occur on three different scales: small, domestic patios inside the individual residential units, mid-sized public courtyards that punctuate the low residential structure, and the large, communal, landscaped space, the paseo. The landscaped lattice folds up vertically; like a carpet; plant growth covers the flat village and climbs up the taller buildings creating an idyllic refuge from the urban surroundings. The paseo, shaded by trees and a vegetation-covered trellis, takes the place of a conventional interior lobby.

This idyllic design brings open green space to a dense urban milieu. The idiosyncratic topology creates a communityoriented social fabric and challenges the prevalent urban social order.

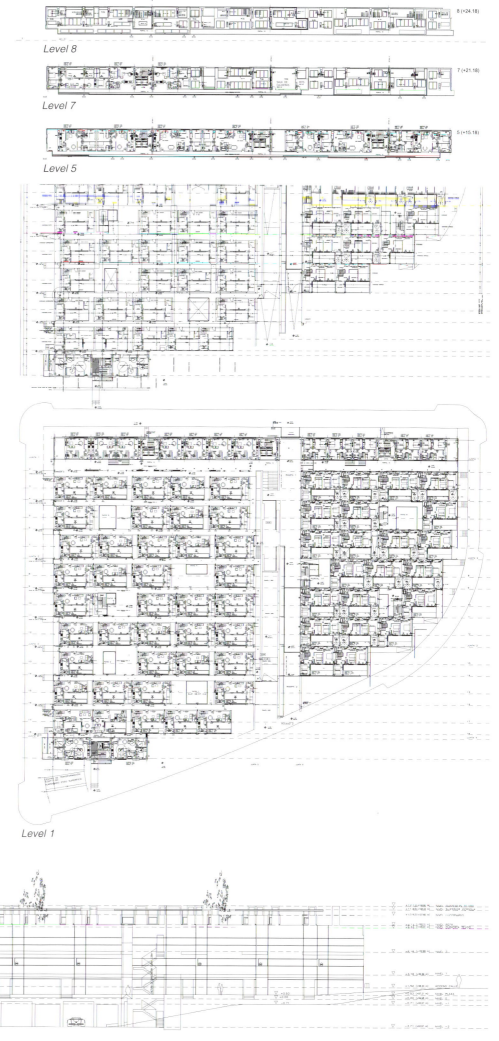

Level 8

Level 7

Level 5

Level 1

Section

North-south main passage　南北に抜ける主通路

Corridor on level 1: north-south passage (right)　2階廊下：右に南北通路

Level 1: east-west passage along seven-story tower
2階：7層のタワー脇の東西に抜ける通路

マドリッド郊外にある平凡で特色のない集合住宅が並ぶ地区に対して，このプロジェクト・タイプが持つ社会的な理想に適合させるために多孔性のタイポロジーを考案した。無性格なユニットから成る高層のハウジングに代わるものとして，風景と集落の形態を結合させ，従来とは根本的に異なる社会的モデルを探求している。一戸建てのヴィラによく見られる特徴を低所得者用ハウジングに接ぎ木することで，スペインの公共集合住宅には通常見られない，ロッジア，グリーン・スペースなどのアメニティがあり，家庭的な尺度を持つ，様々な家族構成に対応した住宅コンプレックスを実現できた。

　オープン・スペースと独特の窪みで構成された，表面を覆うランドスケープの層を，公共的なハウジング計画の画一的な性格を打破するために組み合わせる。基本的な設計概念は，突出した"J"，つまり北側を高層の細長い棟，南側を多層の棟で挟まれた低層の"集落"で構成された建物である。ここには3種類のスケールのオープン・スペースが内包されている。個別の住居ユニット内にある小さく，家庭的なパティオ，低層の住宅棟に穿たれた中間的な大きさの共用の中庭，そして造園された広い共有空間である並木道。植栽を施した格子が縦横に建物を包み，植物は成長するにつれてカーペットのように平坦な"集落"を覆い，高層棟を這い上がって，周囲の都市的な光景から逃れることのできる田園風の憩いの場をつくりあげるだろう。木立や植物に覆われたトレリスが日影をつくる並木道は，型にはまった屋内ロビーに取って代わる。

　この田園風のデザインは，高密度の都市環境に，開放的な緑の空間を運び込む。特異な形態は，コミュニティ指向の公共建築をつくりだし，周囲に広く行き渡っている都市の社会秩序に挑戦する。

View toward stairs to units from north-south main passage
南北に抜ける主通路から各住戸へのアプローチとなる階段を見る

Patio パティオ

2003–09
STEVEN HOLL

LINKED HYBRID
Beijing, China

View from public roof garden of Cinematheque 映画館の屋上庭園より見る

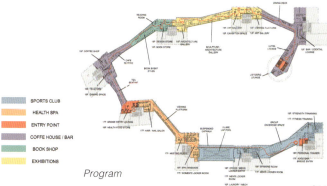

A CINEMATHEQUE
B HOTEL
C POND/PARKING BELOW

Program

Plaza with pond: looking north. Cinematheque on right　池のある広場：北を見る。右は映画館

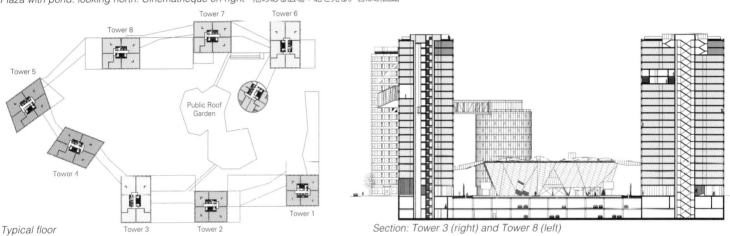

Typical floor

Section: Tower 3 (right) and Tower 8 (left)

The 220,000 square-meter Linked Hybrid complex in Beijing, aims to counter the current privatized urban developments in China by creating a twenty-first century porous urban space, inviting and open to the public from every side. A filmic urban experience of space; around, over and through multifaceted spatial layers, as well as the many passages through the project, make the Linked Hybrid an "open city within a city". The project promotes interactive relations and encourages encounters in the public spaces that vary from commercial, residential, and educational to recreational; a three-dimensional public urban space.

The ground level offers a number of open passages for all people (residents and visitors) to walk through. These passages include "micro-urbanisms" of small scale shops which also activate the urban space surrounding the large central reflecting pond. On the intermediate level of the lower buildings, public roof gardens offer tranquil green spaces, and at the top of the eight residential towers private roof gardens are connected to the penthouses. All public functions on the ground level,—including a restaurant, hotel, Montessori school, kindergarten, and cinema—have connections with the green spaces surrounding and penetrating the project. Elevators displace like a "jump cut" to another series of passages on higher levels. From the 12th to the 18th floor a multi-functional series of skybridges with a swimming pool, a fitness room, a cafe, a gallery, etcetera connects the eight residential towers and the hotel tower, and offers views over the unfolding city. Programmatically this loop aspires to be semi-lattice-like rather than simplistically linear. We hope the public sky-loop and the base-loop will constantly generate random relationships; functioning as social condensers in a special experience of city life to both residents and visitors.

Focused on the experience of passage of the body through space, the towers are organized to take movement, timing and sequence into consideration. The point of view changes with a slight ramp up, a slow right turn. The encircled towers express a collective aspiration; rather than towers as isolated objects or private islands in an increasingly privatized city, our hope is for new "Z" dimension urban sectors that aspire to individuation in urban living while shaping public space.

Geo-thermal wells (655 at 100 meters deep) provide Linked Hybrid with cooling in summer and heating in winter, and make Linked Hybrid one of the largest green residential projects. The large urban space in the center of the project is activated by a grey-water recycling pond with water lilies and grasses in which the cinematheque and the hotel appear to float. In the winter the pool freezes to become an ice-skating rink. The cinematheque is not only a gathering venue but also a visual focus to the area. The cinematheque architecture floats on its reflection in the shallow pond, and projections on its fa-

Overall view from south 南側全景

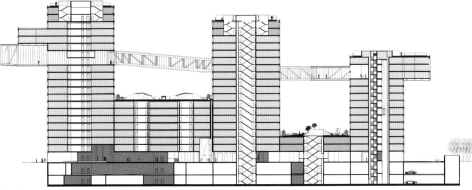

Section: Tower 6 (right), Tower 7 (center) and Tower 8 (left)

cades indicate films playing within. The first floor of the building, with views over the landscape, is left open to the community. The polychrome of Chinese Buddhist architecture inspires a chromatic dimension. The undersides of the bridges and cantilevered portions are colored membranes that glow with projected nightlight and the window jambs have been colored by chance operations based on the 'Book of Changes' with colors found in ancient temples.

The water in the whole project is recycled. This greywater is piped into tanks with ultraviolet filters, and then put back into the large reflecting pond and used to water the landscapes. Re-using the earth excavated from the new construction, five landscaped mounds to the north contain recreational functions. The 'Mound of Childhood', integrated with the kindergarten, has an entrance portal through it. The 'Mound of Adolescence' holds a basketball court, a roller blade and skate board area. In the 'Mound of Middle Age' we find a coffee and tea house (open to all), a Tai Chi platform, and two tennis courts. The 'Mound of Old Age' is occupied with a wine tasting bar and the 'Mound of Infinity' is carved into a meditation space with circular openings referring to infinite galaxies.

Water Efficiency

An estimated 220,000 liters of gray water from all apartment units will be recycled each day and reused for landscape and green roof irrigation, toilet flushing, and rebalancing pond water—resulting in a 41% decrease in potable water usage.

Energy Flows

Linked Hybrid's ground source heat pump system, one of the largest in residential construction, is its most groundbreaking innovation. Shouldering 70% of the complex's yearly heating and cooling load, the system is comprised of 655 geothermal wells, 100 meters below the basement foundation. Additionally, the underground wells have taken the place of above-ground space normally needed for cooling towers, increasing available green areas, minimizing noise pollution and significantly reducing the CO_2 emissions created by traditional heating/cooling methods.

High Performance Building Systems

The project boasts exterior window louvers and low-e coated glass for solar gain and heat control, as well as a high-performance building envelope and integrated slab heating and cooling system.

Indoor Environmental Quality

Linked Hybrid makes use of a technique called displacement ventilation, in which air that is slightly below desired temperature in a room is released from the floor. The cooler air displaces the warmer air, causing it to be released from the room and resulting in a cooler overall space and a fresh breathing environment.

北京における，220,000平米規模のリンクド・ハイブリッド・コンプレックスは，全方位的に人々を迎え入れ，人々に開かれた，21世紀の新しい多孔性の都市空間をつくることによって，中国で現在進んでいる都市開発へ対抗することを目標においている。多面的な空間のレイヤーの周りや，上方やその中を貫通する映像的な都市空間の体験は，プロジェクト全体を通り抜ける数多くの通路と共にリンクド・ハイブリッドを「都市の中の開かれた都市」につくりあげる。プロジェクトは，双方向の関係を押し進め，商業，住居，教育からレクリエーションまで多彩な公共空間内での出会いを促す。それは3次元の都市空間となる。

地上レベルには，すべての人（住民も訪問者も）が隅から隅まで歩き回れる，沢山の開放された通路が巡らされる。これらの通路は，小規模な店舗によるミクロ＝アーバニズムを含み，それらは敷地中央部にある大きなリフレクティング・ポンドの周りの都市空間を活気づける。低層棟の中間レベルでは，パブリックな屋上庭園が静かな緑地を提供し，8棟の住居タワーの頂上ではプライベートな屋上庭園がペントハウスとつながる。レストラン，ホテル，モンテッソーリ法で教える学校，幼稚園，映画館などを含め，地上レベルに置かれたすべての公共施設は，プロジェクトを囲み，浸透する緑地につながる。エレベータはより高いレベルにある一連の別の通路へと映画の「ジャンプカット（急激な場面転換）」のように転置する。12階から18階へ，スイミング・プール，フィットネス・ルーム，カフェ，ギャラリーなどがある多機能な一連のスカイブリッジが8棟の住居タワー，ホテル・タワーを連結し，市街を見晴らせる眺めを提供する。プログラム上は，このループはあまりにも単純な線形よりも半格子状とすることが望ましい。私たちは，公共的な上方のスカイループと基部のベースループが常に無作為な関係を生み出してほしいと願っている。ループは住民にも，訪れる人にも都市生活の特別な体験をもたらす社会的なコンデンサーとして機能する。

タワーは，空間を通り抜けて行く身体の通路体験に照準を合わせ，動き，タイミング，シークエンスを考慮に入れて構成されている。視点はわずかにスロープを上がり，ゆるやかに右へ曲がるにつれて変化する。丸く囲まれたタワーは集合体への願望を表現している。我々が理想とするのは，個別化を強める都市における孤立したオブジェクトや私的な島のようなタワーというよりも，都市空間を形成しながら同時に都市住居としての特徴を生みだす未知の次元の都市セクターなのである。

地熱利用の井戸（100メートルの深さで655基）が，夏と冬の冷暖房設備を提供し，リンクド・ハイブリッドをクリーンエネルギーを使用する，大規模な住宅プロジェクトにする。敷地中央にある大きな都市空間に，シネマテークとホテルが浮かぶように姿を現し，睡蓮や水草が生え，排水を再利用した池によって活気づく。冬にはプールの水面が凍り，アイススケートのリンクとなる。シネマテークは集いの場所であるばかりでなく，このエリアの視覚的な焦点である。シネマテークは浅い池にその姿を反射させながら池の上に浮かび，建物ファサードへの映写は，内部で上映されているフィルムを暗示させる。風景を見晴らせる建物の1階はコミュニティに開放されたまま残される。中国の寺院建築の多色彩飾を施した建築が新しい感覚的な次元を引き起こす。片持ち部分とブリッジの下側は夜間照明の中で光り輝き，窓の竪枠は，古代寺院で見つけた色彩を『易経』に基づいた無作為な運任せの作業によって着色された薄膜で彩色している。

敷地全体で使われる水は再利用される。この雑排水は紫外線フィルターのついたタンクへと管で流され，大きなリフレクティング・ポンドへ戻され，後にランドスケープへの散水として使われる。新しい工事で掘り起こされた土を再利用した，敷地の北側に景観構成された五つのマウンドにはレ

Downward view of pond. Cinematheque with public roof garden and cylindrical volume of Hotel (right) 池を見下す。屋上庭園のある映画館と円形のホテル（右）

クリエーション機能が配される。幼稚園に一体化された「幼児のマウンド」には，入口となる通り抜けの門があり，子供の安全のためにフェンスで囲まれている。「青年期のマウンド」にはバスケットボール・コート，ローラー・ブレードやスケートボード用の場所，もちろん音楽とTVのラウンジもある。「中年期のマウンド」には，カフェと茶店（すべての人に開かれている），太極拳用の壇，2面のテニスコートがある。"老年期のマウンド"はワインのテイスティング・バーと，無限の小宇宙からイメージした円形の開口部付きの，瞑想空間がある"無限のマウンド"で占められる。

節水対策
すべての住戸から1日に排出される220,000リットルの生活排水は，植栽や屋上緑化の散水，トイレの洗浄水，池の水位調整用として再生・再利用される予定である。その結果，上水使用量が41%低減される見込みである。

エネルギー利用
住宅建設としては最大規模の地熱利用式ヒートポンプ・システムは，リンクド・ハイブリッドに採用された最新の先端技術である。複合施設の年間熱負荷の70%を負担するこのシステムは，基礎の地下100メートルに達する655本の地熱井によって構成される。また，この地中井のおかげで，通常であればクーリングタワーの設置に必要とされる地上空間を緑化し，騒音公害を抑え，従来型の冷暖房方式によって排出されるCO_2を大幅に削減する。

ビル・システムの熱効率
太陽熱取得や熱制御のため，断熱性能の高い建築外皮やスラブ一体型の冷暖房システムとともに外部ルーバーやLow-Eガラスが計画されている。

屋内環境品質
リンクド・ハイブリッドでは置換換気という技術が使用されている。そのため，床面からは目標室温よりもやや低く設定された空気が吹き出される。冷気と暖気が置換されることで，排気が促され，空間全般の室温を低く保ち，新鮮で快適な環境がもたらされる。

Evening view: Tower 1 (left) and Tower 2 (right)　夕景：タワー1（左）とタワー2（右）

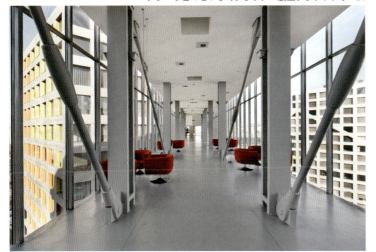

Bridge between Tower 3 and Tower 4: viewing platform
タワー3と4をつなぐブリッジ：展望プラットフォーム

Bridge between Tower 2 and Tower 3: swimming pool below (right)
タワー2と3をつなぐブリッジ：下階はスイミング・プール（右）

2003–11
FRANK O. GEHRY

8 SPRUCE STREET*
New York, New York, U.S.A.
at present: New York by Gehry

View from Brooklyn Bridge Park　ブルックリン・ブリッジ・パークより見る

Eight Spruce Street is located on a 44,000 sq.ft. site in lower Manhattan. The building is a 76-story mixed-use building, which houses a pre-kindergarten through eighth grade public school, office space for the New York Downtown Hospital, and over nine hundred residential units. The site sits between Spruce Street on the North and Beekman Street on the South. There are through block plazas on both the East and West side of the building. The West Plaza creates a landscaped setting for a porte cochere that gives car and pedestrian access to the residential lobby.

Gehry began by using the classical proportions of New York City towers and the traditional setback rules which have created the tall wedding cake designs typical in the city. He used these guidelines to create the initial massing of the building. Gehry then developed the design to accommodate bay windows which the client requested in each unit. Rather than align the bay windows vertically, he moved them slightly from floor-to-floor and adjusted their sizes from unit-to-unit. Gehry made many studies of this and realized that it had the look of fabric draping over the building, so he developed the design to accentuate this effect. Seven sides of the tower have this configuration, while the south side of the tower is sheared into a flat plane that con-

View from northwest 北西より見る

trasts the curvature of the other facades and strengthens the sculptural composition. The flat side is essential to the power of the building.

The tower is clad in flat and undulating stainless steel panels. At the base of the tower is a simple five storey brick podium, which was designed to be in the spirit of the neighboring buildings.

Due to the undulating facade each floor of the tower and each residential unit on the seven undulating sides will have a different configuration. Gehry Partners has designed the apartment interiors to take best advantage of these unique conditions, with large windows framing views and creating window seats on some of the large window sills that are created by the movement of the wall from floor to floor. The bay windows also afford residents the opportunity to step out past the plane of the exterior wall in what Gehry calls "stepping into space" and to have the feeling of being suspended over the whole of Manhattan.

The apartments range in size from 450-square-foot studios to 1,700-square-foot 3 bedroom apartments at the top of the tower. Gehry Partners has planned these units to maximize the efficiency of the plans while creating homes with beautiful finishes and light filled rooms. An enclosed swimming pool and other residential amenities are on the roof of the podium.

The building is in a part of lower Manhattan with few other towers. It is close to City Hall and its beautiful park. The landmark Woolworth Building by Cass Gilbert and the Brooklyn Bridge are its closest neighbors. At over 860' tall it will be a prominent addition to the New York City skyline and will be the tallest residential building in Manhattan upon completion. It will not only be a distinctive addition to the city skyline but also provide much needed space for the New York community. It could only have been built in Manhattan.

Aerial view from west 西側上空より見る

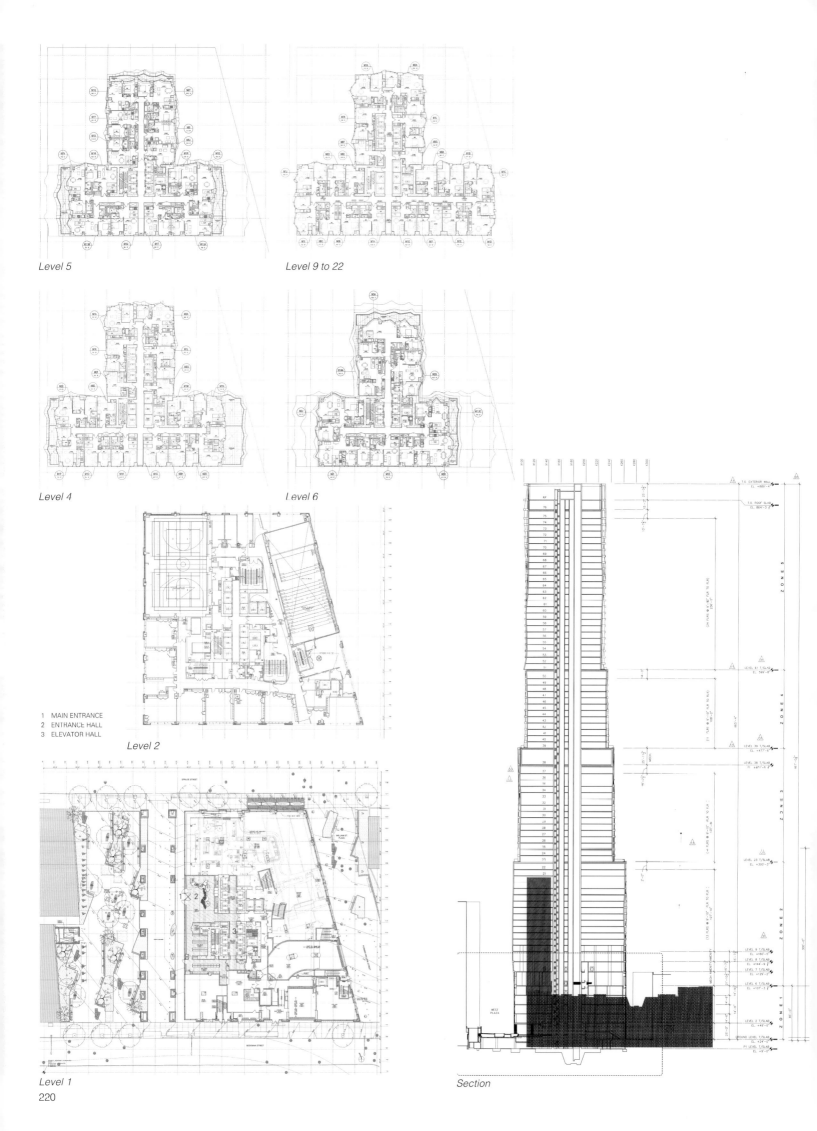

Level 5

Level 9 to 22

Level 4

Level 6

1 MAIN ENTRANCE
2 ENTRANCE HALL
3 ELEVATOR HALL

Level 2

Level 1

Section

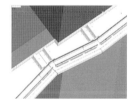

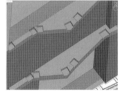

Detail: wall system

Wall mock-up

Upper part of north elevation　北面上部

221

Main entrance メイン・エントランス

Entrance hall エントランス・ホール

Model room モデル・ルーム△▷

エイト・スプルス・ストリートはローワー・マンハッタンにある44,000平方フィート（約4,090平米）の敷地に立つ。この建物は76階建ての複合施設で，保育園児から8年生までの児童のためのパブリックスクールや，ニューヨーク・ダウンタウン病院のオフィス，そして900戸を越える住居ユニットを内包する。敷地は北側のスプルス・ストリートと，南側のビークマン・ストリートの間に位置する。建物の東と西の両側には一部ブロックを貫通する広場がある。西側広場には，車と歩行者が居住者用ロビーにアクセスするために造園された車寄せがある。

ゲーリーは，ニューヨーク市にある高層タワーの古典的な形状と，この街で一般的な背の高いウェディングケーキ状の伝統的なセットバック規制を利用することから設計を始めた。彼はここで得られた設計指針を用いて建物の初期ヴォリュームを導いている。次にゲーリーは，クライアントが各住居ユニットに要求したベイ・ウィンドウを組み入れるためにデザインを展開した。彼は各戸のベイ・ウィンドウを垂直方向に一直線に揃えるのではなく，これらを階層間で少しずつずらし，各住戸間でそのサイズを調整している。ゲーリーはこの点に関して多くの検討を重ねるうち，その形状が建物を覆う布の襞のように見える点に気づいて，この効果を強調するアイディアを発展させた。七つの面においてそのような輪郭とし，タワー南面はフラットにせん断し，湾曲した他のファサード面とコントラストを成すことで彫塑的な構成を強めている。フラットな面は建物の力強さを示すのに欠かせない要素だ。

このタワーは，平面や波形にうねるステンレス・スティール製パネルで被覆されている。タワー基部は単純なレンガ積みの腰石で5層分を覆い，周辺の建物の雰囲気に沿った設計としている。

起伏するファサード面であるため，タワーの各

階と七つの起伏した面に配置した各住居ユニットは，それぞれ異なる構成となった。ゲーリー・パートナーズは，こうしたユニークな状況を最適化するにあたり，景観を紡ぎだす大窓や，階層間の壁面の変化が生み出す大開口の枠に組み込まれる窓枠シートといった，アパートの内装を提案した。ベイ・ウィンドウについても，ゲーリーが言うところの「空間に足を踏み入れる」かのように，居住者が外壁面よりも外側に出て，まるでマンハッタン上空から吊り下げられたような感覚を得る機会を提供している。

アパートは，最小450平方フィート（約42平米）のスタジオユニットから，タワー最上部の最大1,700平方フィート（約158平米）の3ベッドルーム・アパートで構成されている。ゲーリー・パートナーズは，プランに関しては各ユニットで最大限に効率化しながら，美しい仕上げや光にあふれる部屋をつくり出した。屋内スイミングプールや，その他の居住者向け利便設備類はタワー基部の最上階に置いた。

この建物は，周辺に立つ幾つかのタワーと共にローワー・マンハッタンの一部となる。シティーホールと，その美しい公園にもほど近い。キャス・ギルバートによるウールワース・ビルディングやブルックリン・ブリッジなどのランドマークが，タワーの隣人として最も近いものとなる。860フィート（約260メートル）を越える高さを持ち，ニューヨーク市の高層スカイラインの中でも突出した参入者となるこのタワーは，完成時にはマンハッタンで最も背の高い居住向け建築となる。街のスカイラインに対して個性的な追加物となるだけでなく，ニューヨークのコミュニティで強く求められている空間を生みだすことになる。これは，マンハッタンという地でのみ成立可能な建築と言うことが出来るだろう。

Upward view　壁面見上げ

Terrace　テラス

2004–07
JEAN NOUVEL

40 MERCER LODGEMENTS
New York, New York, U.S.A.

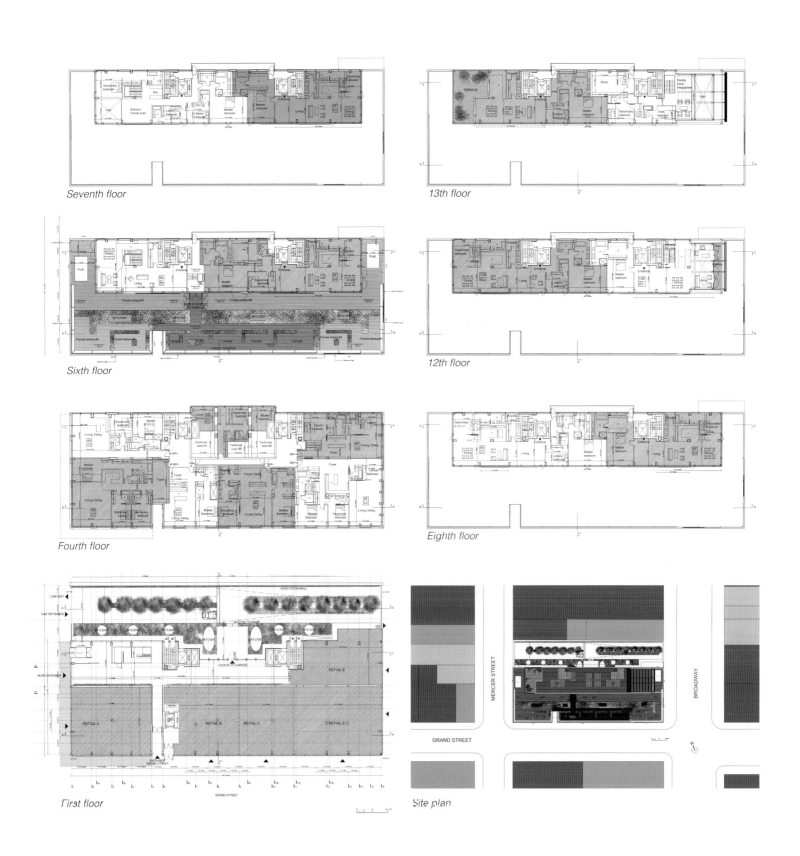

View from corner of Broadway and Grand Street

Night view of north entrance　北側エントランス夜景

Entrance hall　エントランス・ホール

Entrance hall: retail on right　エントランス・ホール：右は店舗

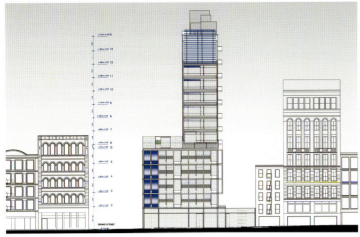

East elevation

West elevation

South elevation

North elevation

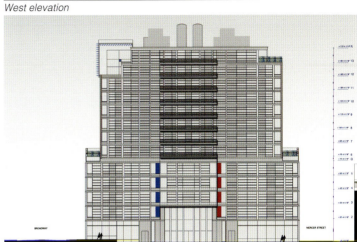

Section A

The Soho project was founded on two propositions which were elaborated by the qualities offered by the site. It has the particularity of leaving three of its sides free, which is a rare opportunity in New York. The most obvious reaction would have been to lean the building against the neighbouring wall but I preferred to pull it away from the wall. Hotels are always very functional (lifts, fire exits...), and I wanted to take the staircases one sees on all the New York facades to propose an interpretation: I conceived a very narrow staircase, a kind of ladder which spans the first five levels of the hotel. The continuity between this fractured volume and the neighbouring block is ensured by a swimming-pool. Installed in the basement, it follows, along all its length, the neighbouring wall which seems to dive in. From above to below, by length and width, an effect of transparency dresses or undresses the hotel and reveals its anatomy. A series of games on the typology of the rooms by matter and the color of the glass combines with the general structure. I exploited the multiple qualities of glass to reply to the aspirations of the hotel clients. The problem of the hotel room in an urban environment is of a paradoxical nature. We have to preserve a certain mystery, and protect the intimacy of the occupants, but they also want to make the most of the privileged location of the building in the city. I play on the precision of the graphics and on the nature of what is a hotel room. The glass changes from transparency to opacity; I used colored glass, a very deep red which almost seems black from the outside. Depending on the time of day, the building changes: from a massive object with sharp contours, it tends towards dematerialization, the frontiers between inside and outside melt away. The project is articulated, in this play on the matter of the glass used, between appearance and disappearance of matter: it lends an erotic character to the architecture.

Penthouse: upward view of louver　ペントハウス：ルーバー見上げ

Roof terrace on sixth floor and penthouse with louver
6階，ルーフテラスとルーバーのあるペントハウス

Elevator hall　エレベータ・ホール

Panorama from housing unit　住戸からのパノラマ

Housing unit: bathroom　住戸：浴室

Housing unit: kitchen　住戸：キッチン

Downward view of roof terrace on sixth floor　6階，ルーフテラス見下ろし

ソーホー・プロジェクトは，敷地が備えている特質から精巧に練り上げられた二つの提案に基づいている。敷地は三方が通りに面して開いており，これはニューヨークでは稀な条件である。最も常識的な対応は建物を隣接する壁に向かってもたせかけることだろうが，私は壁から引き離す方を選んだ。ホテルというのは常に非常に機能的（エレベータ，火災用避難口など）なもので，私は一つの解釈を提案するために，ニューヨークのあらゆるファサードに見られる階段をとりあげてみたいと思った。ホテル低層部の5層を架け渡す，梯子のような非常に幅の狭い階段を思いついた。この分断された建物と隣のブロックとの間の連続性はスイミング・プールで確保される。地階に設置されたプールは，その全長が隣の壁に沿って続き，付近の壁がプールにもぐり込んでいるように見える。上から下まで，長さと幅いっぱいに，透明性がもたらす効果をホテルに付けたり外したりして，その骨格を明らかにする。材料やガラスの色を用いた，部屋のタイポロジーに対する一連のゲームが全体構造を結びつける。ホテル客の願望に応えるために，ガラスの多種多様な特性を利用した。

都市環境内でホテルの部屋が抱える問題は，その逆説的な性格である。ある種の神秘性を保たねばならず，客の居心地のよさも守らねばならないが，ホテル側はまた，この街の中での建物の特権的なロケーションを最大限に活用することを必要としている。私は，グラフィックの精緻さとホテルの部屋というものの本質についてゲームを演じてみた。ガラスは透明なものから不透明なものへ変化する。外から見るとほとんど黒に見える深紅色の着色ガラスを用いた。1日の時間帯によって建物は変貌する。鋭い輪郭を持つ量感のある物体から，物質的性格を失い，内側と外側の境界はしだいに消え去る。建物は，使われているガラスという物質，その物質が現れ消えて行くという戯れの中で，明瞭にかたちづくられる。それは建築に官能的な性格を付与する。

Sixth floor: roof terrace　6階：ルーフテラス

2005–08
BIG/BJARKE INGELS

THE MOUNTAIN
Copenhagen, Denmark

How do you combine the splendours of the suburban backyard with the social intensity of urban density?

The Mountain is the 2nd generation of the VM-Houses—same client, same size and same street. The program, however, is 2/3 parking and 1/3 living. What if the parking area became the base upon which to place terraced housing—like a concrete hillside covered by a thin layer of housing, cascading from the 11th floor to the street edge? Rather than doing two separate buildings next to each other—a parking and a housing block—we decided to merge the two functions into a symbiotic relationship. The parking area needs to be connected to the street, and the homes require sunlight, fresh air and views, thus all apartments have roof gardens facing the sun, amazing views and parking on the 10th floor. The Mountain appears as a suburban neighbourhood of garden homes flowing over a 10-storey building—suburban living with urban density.

The roof gardens consist of a terrace and a garden with plants changing character according to the changing seasons. The building has a huge watering system which maintains the roof gardens. The only thing that separates the apartment and the garden is a glass façade with sliding doors to provide light and fresh air.

The residents of the 80 apartments will be the first in Orestaden to have the possibility of parking directly outside their homes. The gigantic parking area contains 480 parking spots and a sloping elevator that moves along the mountain's inner walls. In some places the ceiling height is up to 16 meters which gives the impression of a cathedral-like space.

The north and west facades are covered by perforated aluminium plates, which let in air and light to the parking area. The holes in the facade form a huge reproduction of Mount Everest. At day the holes in the aluminium plates will appear black on the bright aluminium, and the gigantic picture will resemble that of a rough rasterized photo. At night time the facade will be lit from the inside and appear as a photo negative in different colours as each floor in the parking area has different colours.

The Mountain is located in Orestad city and offer the best of two worlds: closeness to the hectic city life in the centre of Copenhagen, and the tranquillity characteristic of suburban life.

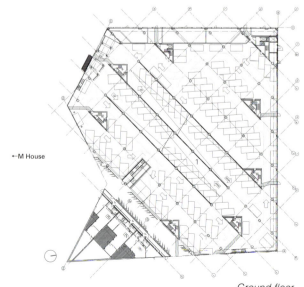

Ground floor

The Mountain (right) and M House (left, pp.192-197) ザ・マウンテン（右）とMハウス（左, pp.192-197）

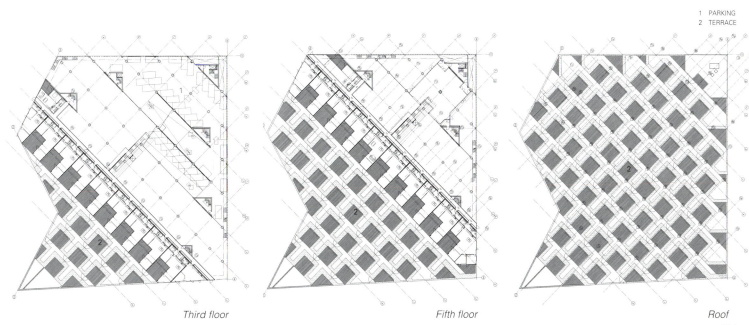

1 PARKING
2 TERRACE

Third floor   *Fifth floor*   *Roof*

Looking south from terrace. M House on right　テラスより南を見る。右はMハウス

View from northeast: stepped apartment units with parking beneath　北東より見る：段状の住戸ユニットの真下に駐車場がある

郊外の美しさと都市的密度がもたらす力強さを，いかにして融合するか？

　「ザ・マウンテン」は，「VMハウス」と同じクライアントからの依頼である。この二つの建築は同じ通りに面しており，規模についても同程度だが，プログラムの面では大きく異なる。「ザ・マウンテン」は3分の2をパーキング，3分の1を住居が占めている。我々は，パーキングエリアをテラスハウスが載る基礎の部分にすることを考えた。11階から足元の通りまで滝のように段々と降りてくる，住居の薄いレイヤーに覆われたコンクリートの丘のような建築である。パーキング・ブロックと住居ブロックというように機能によって建物を分離するのではなく，二つの機能を統合し，両者の間に共生関係を形成しようとした。パーキングエリアは通りとの接続性，住居は日照，通風，眺望が必要である。そこで，各住戸にはルーフガーデンを設けた。「ザ・マウンテン」は10階建ての建物の上を流れる庭園住宅の集合体，都市的密度をもった郊外住宅の集合体としてあらわれる。

　ルーフガーデンは，季節の移り変わりに応じて表情を変える庭とテラスからなる。巨大な水供給システムが建物全体に施されている。光と空気を通すスライディング・ドアをもつガラス・ファサードだけが住居と庭を分離している。巨大なパーキングエリアには480台分の駐車スペースがあり，山の内壁に沿って斜めに傾いたエレベータが設置される。天井高が16メートルに達する場所もあり，あたかも大聖堂の空間のような印象を与える。

　北面ファサードと西面ファサードは多孔アルミニウムプレートに覆われ，光と空気をパーキングエリアに取り入れる。ファサードにあけられた孔によって，建物の表面にエベレストの姿を浮かび上がらせる。日中は，アルミニウムにあけられた孔が明るく輝くアルミニウムとコントラストをなし，ラスタライズした粗い写真のような表情を見せる。夜になると，ファサードは逆に内側から照らされ，異なる色彩をもつパーキングエリアと同様に，ポジとネガを反転した写真のようになる。

　オレスタッド市にあるこの「ザ・マウンテン」は，コペンハーゲン中心部でのあわただしい都市生活からも離れることなく，郊外生活に特徴的な静謐さを兼ね備えた建築である。

View from M house toward the Mountain　Mハウスよりザ・マウンテンを見る

Parking: each level has different colors　駐車場：各階で色が異なる △▽

233

Stepped terraces　段状のテラス

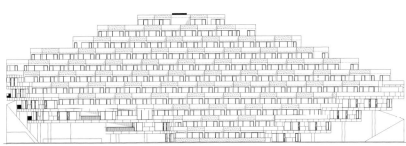
Southeast elevation　S=1:1000

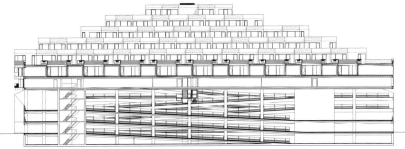
Section　S=1:1000

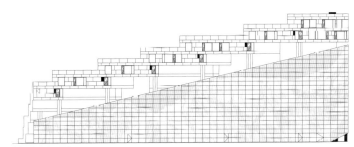
North elevation

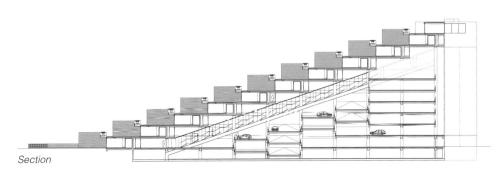
Section

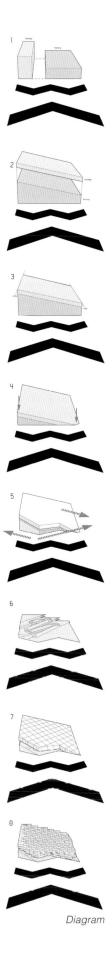
Diagram

Diagram
Volume of residence and parking. With shaping its plan same as M House, by setting the volume of parking as inclined on from south to north higher, dwelling above can obtain individual views and terraces

ダイアグラム
居住棟と駐車場棟のヴォリューム。平面形状をMハウス同様にするだけでなく、駐車場を北側に向かって階段状にすることで、その上のアパートは南側に向けた段状になり、各住戸は独立したテラスと風景を手に入れる

Unit plans S=1:500

◁△▽ Unit on top floor (duplex)　最上階の住戸（デュプレックス）

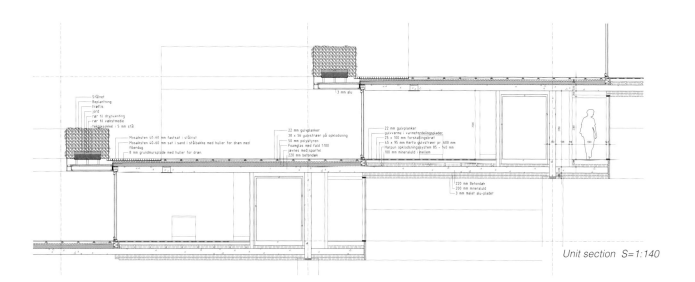
Unit section S=1:140

2005–11
SMITH-MILLER + HAWKINSON

405-427 WEST 53RD STREET "THE DILLON"
New York, New York, U.S.A.

Street view on south 南側の通りより見る

Partial south elevation 道路側の南面

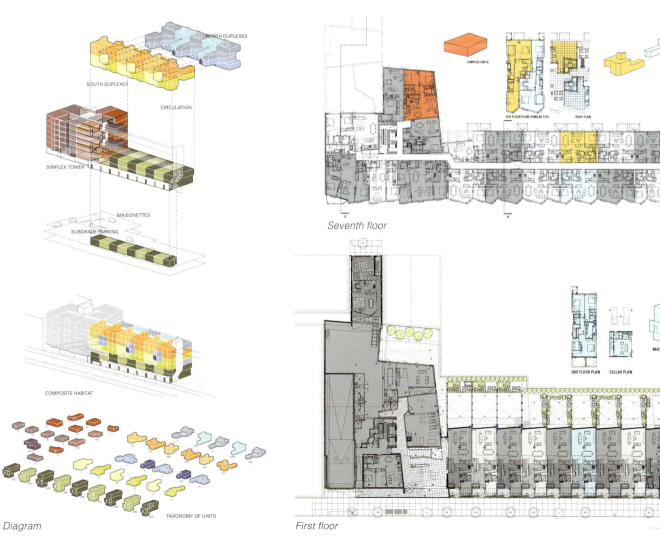

Diagram

Seventh floor

First floor

North elevation 北面

New York has often served as incubator for innovative residential design; from the first cooperative developed by the Brooklyn based Norwegian community, to the ubiquitous NYC brownstone block, and the descendents of Le Corbusier's "Ville Radieuse", in the form of Gordon Bunshaft's Manhattan House, James Freed's Kip's Bay, and Oscar Stonoroff's NYU Housing. More recent project progeny include Jean Nouvel's Grand Street lofts, Richard Meier's and Charles Gwathmey's downtown towers, as well as Pauson's Gramercy Park and Dubledaum's TriBeca experiments.

Hell's Kitchen, now known as Clinton North, enjoys remarkable urban assets; close proximity to NYC's mid-town, Rockefeller Center, MoMA, the theater district, the Heart Building, AOL-Time Warner, Central Park, the subways (C, E, 1, 2, 3, N, and R) and the West Side Highway.

While 405-9 W 53rd finds precedent in the city's past, it projects a dense fabric for city living, melding maisonette, duplex, triplex and studio apartments in a cosmopolitan weave. Apartment tower flats, skip-stop duplex, and triplex maisonette units are all served by street front and below grade self-park facilities.

As an extensive low rise and mid-block project, the building replaces currently open parking lots and derelict structures with an optimistic premise drawn in part from Jane Jacob's observations of city life (and tempered by a competitive design environment). The maisonettes' small street-side forecourts buffer domestic activity while affording direct street access to a full width ground floor and garden.

Stacking skip-stop floor thru units on maisonettes and below grade parking garage creates a building section of remarkable economy. Most units enjoy southern street side and northern court exposure with natural floor-through ventilation.

The folded fifty-third street facade offers views across and along the street, westward to the Hudson River and eastward for early morning light. Open plan flats, duplex and

Maisonette unit: sectional perspective

maisonette units capitalize on available light and view. The project has an informal quality that seems to step down the street.

Given the evolving nature of the district and its restrictive zoning, we thought to offer different dwelling types. With a wide spectrum of unit types (footprints and volumes) we were able to substantially decrease the project's loss factor while offering a much needed variety.

Our thru-block site hosts both the New York customary residential tower with repeating floor plans and an a-typical model; a slab or bar building with a combination of maisonettes, skip stop duplex and skip stop triplexes with roof top cabanas all served by underground self parking facilities.

Diversity of dwelling types may collectively reflect the social organization of a neighborhood resulting in a seemingly casual and informal appearance.

Dressed in an articulate and detailed skin, the assemblage projects a new typology for urban living.

Henry Smith-Miller

Maisonette unit: court on north　メゾネット・ユニット：北側の中庭

Maisonette unit: living/dining room　メゾネット・ユニット：居間／食堂

Maisonette unit: view from entrance　メゾネット・ユニット：玄関より見る

South duplex unit: living/dining room 南側デュプレックス・ユニット：居間／食堂

South duplex unit: bedroom 南側デュプレックス・ユニット：寝室

ニューヨークは，しばしば革新的な住宅デザインの孵化器の役割を果たしてきた。

ブルックリンを拠点にするノルウェー人コミュニティによって発展した初期の共同住宅にはじまり，ニューヨーク市のあらゆる場所でみられるブラウンストーンの街区，ル・コルビュジエの「ヴィラ・ラデューズ（輝く都市）」から派生した建築まで至り，ゴードン・バンシャフトのマンハッタン・ハウス，ジェームズ・フリードのキップス・ベイ，オスカー・ストロノフのNYUハウジングのような例がある。より最近のプロジェクトでは，ジャン・ヌヴェルのグランド・ストリートのロフト，リチャード・マイヤーやチャールズ・グワスミーによるダウンタウンの高層建築に引き継がれており，ポーソンのグラマシー・パーク，ダブルダムによるトライベッカでの実験も含まれる。

現在はクリントン・ノースとして知られるヘルズ・キッチンは，すばらしい都市の資源に恵まれている。すぐ近くにはニューヨーク市のミッドタウンやロックフェラー・センター，MoMA（ニューヨーク近代美術館），劇場街，ハースト・タワー，AOLタイム・ワーナー，セントラル・パーク，地下鉄（路線Ｃ，Ｅ，１，２，３，Ｎ，Ｒ）とウエストサイド・ハイウェイがある。

「405-9 W53rd」はこの街の過去に焦点を当て，メゾネット，２層，３層，ワンルームの部屋を織り交ぜたコスモポリタンな構成による，都市生活のための密度の高い仕組みを提案している。高層住宅のフラット，２～３層のメゾネットのユニットはすべて前面の道路に面し，下階に駐車場を備えている。

広大な低層のミッドブロックの計画として，ジェーン・ジェイコブスの都市生活へのまなざしを部分的に取り入れながら（またデザイン性を競う環境に刺激されて），建物は屋外駐車場と放置され

1 ROOF DECK
2 LIVING/DINING/KITCHEN
3 MASTER BEDROOM
4 BEDROOM
5 CORRIDOR
6 ENTRY
7 MEDIA ROOM
8 PARKING
9 COMMERCIAL UNIT
10 MECHANICAL

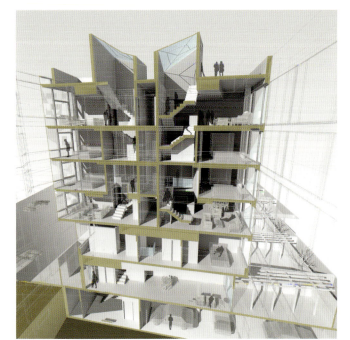
Sectional perspective

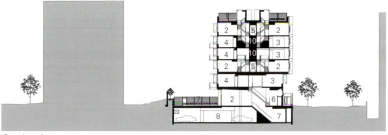
Section A

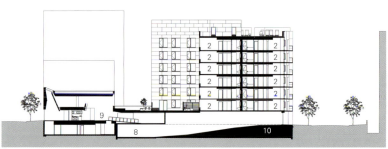
Section B

た構造体からゆったりとした空間に取って代わった。通りに面したメゾネットの小さな前庭は，内部の生活の緩衝となると同時に，道路側の地上面や庭へ間口いっぱいに開放されている。

階をまたぐ複層のユニットを下階の駐車場に積み上げると，建物の断面は非常に経済的になる。ほとんどのユニットは南側の道路と北側の中庭の景色を楽しむ事ができ，床からの自然換気が可能である。53番街に面したジグザグのファサードによって，道路の向こうや道路沿いを望むことができる。西にはハドソン川への眺望があり，東からは朝日が入る。ワンルーム，2層，メゾネットのユニットは採光と眺望を可能な限り活かしている。

この計画は，通りへ降り立ったような親しみやすい雰囲気がある。

この地区の発展的な性質とゾーニングの制限を考慮して，私たちは異なる住居タイプを提案することを考えた。さまざまな種類（平面形状，ヴォリューム）のユニットタイプが集合して，計画の実質的な損失を抑えながら，それよりずっと必要とされている多様性を提供することを可能にした。

ブロックを横断することで，平面計画を反復するニューヨークの慣例的な高層住宅とスラブや鉄骨によるメゾネット，デュプレックス，ペントハウス付きのトリプレックスを組み合せた不規則なモデルを両立し，全てが地下の駐車スペースに接続している。

多様な住居タイプが集合することで周辺の社会構造に影響を与えるので，一見してカジュアルで親しみやすい外観となった。

明快かつ詳細に設計された皮膜に覆われ，集合体は都市生活の新しいタイポロジーを提示している。

（ヘンリー・スミス＝ミラー）

South duplex unit (with roof terrace): living/dining room
南側デュプレックス・ユニット（ルーフテラス付き）：居間／食堂

South duplex unit (with roof terrace): staircase to roof terrace on left
南側デュプレックス・ユニット（ルーフテラス付き）：左はルーフテラスへの階段

South duplex unit (with roof terrace): roof terrace
南側デュプレックス・ユニット（ルーフテラス付き）：ルーフテラス

2006–09
MICHAEL MALTZAN

NEW CARVER APARTMENTS
Los Angeles, California, U.S.A.

View from west: main entrance on left 西より見る：左にメイン・エントランス

Just south of Los Angeles' fast-growing downtown and immediately adjacent to the I-10 freeway, the New Carver Apartments explores how architecture can create new possibilities for its highly vulnerable, dramatically under-served residents as well as for Los Angeles as a whole. The project's 97 units provide permanent housing for formerly homeless elderly and disabled residents, a place for solace, support, and individual growth in the face of the city's chronic homeless problem. By incorporating communal spaces—kitchens, dining areas, gathering spaces and gardens—into the Carver's raised form, as well as medical and social service support facilities into the plinth beneath, the project encourages its residents to not only reconnect with each other but also with the world outside its doors.

Confronted with a significant level of ambient noise from passing automobiles, the form creates a sound buffer by minimizing the building's area directly opposite the freeway; smaller-scale facets position unit windows perpendicular to the direction of sound, further shielding the units themselves. The facade underscores the relationship between the building and the freeway, creating a subtle pattern of light and shadow further animated by the illumination of passing cars. As automobiles pass from east to west, the building's facade transforms itself as its saw tooth facets open to view.

Viewed from the freeway and the street, the project's faceted form articulates the scale of the individual units within, expressing the dynamic relationship between an urban fabric composed of individual lives, the texture of our collective experience, and the speed of the freeway. At street level a series of lines trace the street inwards, defining primary circulation paths, organizing program spaces, and creating views deep into and across the block. The architecture urges residents to connect with the urban context at multiple scales and from multiple vantage points throughout the building. The screened central courtyard connects vertically to the natural sky; a grand stair gestures down towards the urban fabric of the ground floor, drawing the courtyard space across the lobby and into the street. At the top floor, a partially-covered terrace creates dramatic views of the downtown skyline. Visual and perceptual connections to the local landscape abound at multiple scales, drawing out the rich texture of the social program and sitting it within the expansive perspective of the architecture.

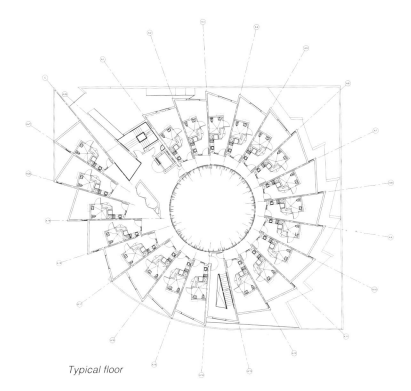

Typical floor

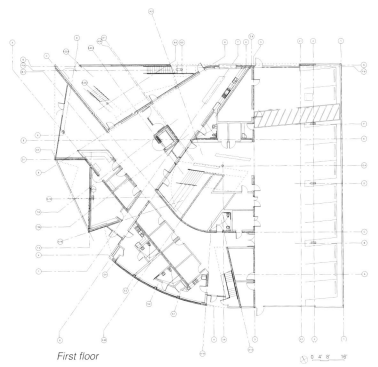

First floor

View from southeast: freeway on left 南東より見る：左は高速道路

Exploded exterior elevations

243

View from north　北より見る

Terrace on top floor　最上階のテラス

Cafeteria 食堂

Corridor 廊下

Lobby ロビー

Main entrance メイン・エントランス

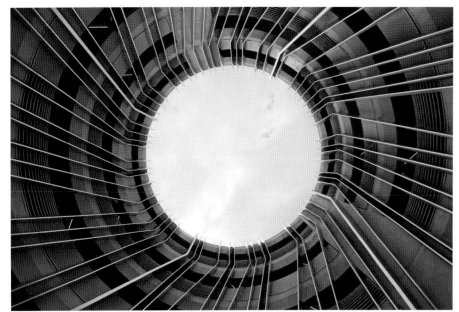
Upward view of courtyard 中庭の見上げ

Central courtyard 中庭

このアパートメントは，ロサンゼルスの中で急速な発展を遂げている商業地区のすぐ南側に位置しており，高速道 I-10 号の脇に立っている。ここでは，社会的に極めて弱い立場にありながら，不十分な扱いしか受けられない住民たち，およびロサンゼルスのまち全体に対して，如何にして建築が新たな可能性を創造できるかを追求している。計画された97戸の住居は，以前ホームレスだった高齢者と身体障害者に恒久的な住まいを提供し，この街が慢性的なホームレス問題に直面する中で必要とする慰めの場，支援の場，そして個人の成長のための場も用意しているのである。上に向かって立ち上げられたヴォリューム内には，台所や食堂，集会室や庭などの公共スペースが収められ，その下にあたる基壇部には医療や社会サービス支援のための施設を収める。こうして，このプロジェクトは居住者同士の間の交流を改めて生みだすだけでなく，ドアの外に広がる世界とも彼等が繋がれるようにと導いている。

通過する自動車の激しい騒音との対面は避けられないため，高速道路と直に面する建物の面積を最小限に抑える形状にすることで，音の緩衝帯をつくり出している―小さな切子状になった部分によって，騒音の出る方向に対して住戸の窓が直行するため，住戸自体が騒音から守られるのである。このファサードは，通過する車の照明でより一層強められる光と影による繊細なパターンを浮かび上がらせながら，建物と高速道路との関係性を強調している。車が東から西へ通り過ぎると，その鋸刃の切子状の面が視界に開けて建物のファサードが変容する。

高速道路と一般の通りから見ると，この建物の切子状の形態は，内包された各住戸のスケールを明解に示している。さらに，個人の生活によって組み立てられている都市の構造や，我々が蓄積してきた経験から生まれるテクスチャー，そして高速道のスピード感，それらの間に流れるダイナミックな関係性も表している。主要動線を決めながら，求められているプログラムを収め，さらに街区を超えた遠方へも視界が抜けるように，地上にある道路レベルでは道路を内側に引き込むような連続するラインを描いている。この建築は，建物内に複数用意した見晴らしの良い場所から，居住者が都市のコンテクストとつながれるように促している。スクリーンで覆われた中庭は，垂直方向に自然の空と繋がる―大階段は，都市的な構成による地上階へ下りる様を体現し，ロビー越しの中庭の空間を引き寄せながら道路レベルへと繋がる。最上階にある，部分的に覆われたテラスからは，商業地区のスカイラインというダイナミックな風景を見渡せる。社会的プログラムの豊かなテクスチャーを引き出して，この建物の多角的な視野の中にそのテクスチャーを位置づけながら，様々なスケールにおいて周囲の景観と視覚的かつ知覚的なつながりを多くつくり出すのである。

Downward view 見下ろし

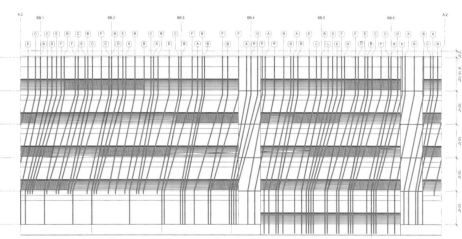
Courtyard elevation

Corridor around central void 中央の吹抜け廻りの廊下

Corridor 廊下

2007–12
ALBERTO KALACH

REFORMA 27
Mexico City, México

The residential tower located in Reforma 27 was designed in collaboration with ICA following the classic principles expressed 2000 years ago by Vitruvius; Venustas, Firmitas and Utilitas.

The structure, essential to every tower, is utilized as the very expression of the building: it is its support, container of spaces, and facade, which creates the thermal protection and intimacy necessary for the apartments. The completely open floor plan allows the distribution of 10 different modular apartments ranging from 40 m² to 240 m².

Below, a high comercial portico ties the tower with Paseo de la Reforma, above, a greenhouse with tropical plants and a pool with a hallucinatory subaquatic mural painted by Marco Kalach, relates it with the city and its volcanoes.

Main entrance メイン・エントランス △▽

◁ View from east 東より見る

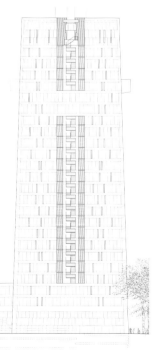

West elevation S=1:1200

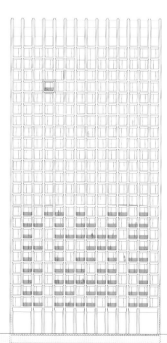

South elevation

Typical floor

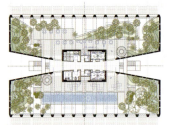
Level 24: swimming pool and greenhouse

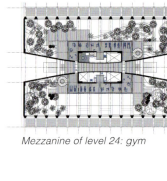
Mezzanine of level 24: gym

Typical parking level (underground) S=1:1200

Access level

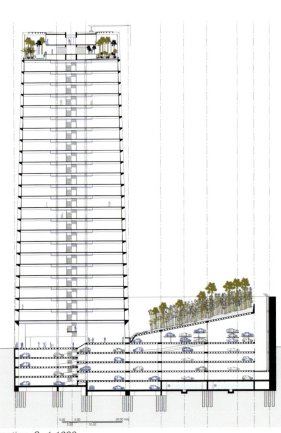
Section S=1:1200

Garden on northwest 北西側庭園

レフォルマ通り27番地に建つこの高層集合住宅はICAと協働し，2,000年前にウィトルウィウスが示した古典原理"美・強・用"にならって設計された。

どの高層建築にとってもそうであるが，構造はその建物の本質であり根幹となるものである。時にそれは建物を支える支持体であり，部屋を納める箱であり，また熱を遮り集合住宅に必要とされるくつろげる内部空間をつくり出すファサードでもある。完全なオープンプランをとることによって40平方メートルから240平方メートルまでの10タイプの異なる部屋を配置することが可能となった。下階では商店の入ったポルティコがレフォルマ通りと建物を結びつけ，上階には熱帯植物の温室や，またマルコ・カラチによる街と火山をモチーフにした幻想的な水中画が描かれたプールがある。

Pilotis at main entrance　メイン・エントランスのピロティ

Entrance lobby　エントランス・ロビー

Elevator hall on level 24 with skylight
レベル24，スカイライトから光の差し込むエレベータ・ホール

Exterior staircase 外部階段

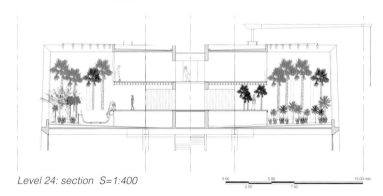
Level 24: section S=1:400

△▷ *Interior of apartment* 住戸内部

Swimming pool スイミング・プール

Pool side プールサイド

Glazed bridge on mezzanine of greenhouse
グリーンハウス，中2階，ガラスのブリッジ

2008–14
JEAN NOUVEL

ONE CENTRAL PARK
Sydney, New South Wales, Australia

View from northeast 北東より見る

Upward view of north elevation　北面見上げ

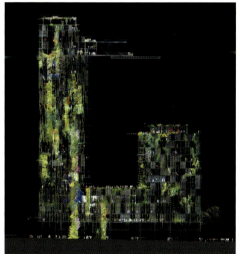

North elevation

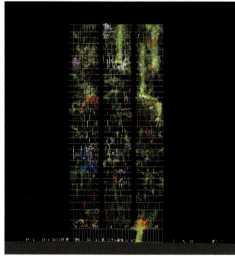

East elevation S=1:2000

Section S=1:1000

One Central Park (OCP), by developers Frasers Property and Sekisui House, is an innovative and environmentally ambitious landmark project within the redevelopment of the Carlton & United Brewery site near Central Station in Sydney. The overall planning intent is to adhere to the highest standards of sustainable residential design under the Australian Green Star rating system and support the vision of an environmentally responsible future for the city. Unfortunately, mere Green Star compliance often tends to be barely perceptible. In order to make the two towers of OCP visibly greener, the design takes a broader approach to carbon conscious design and exceeds the mere fulfillment of Green Star requirements. With the help of two unusual technologies—hydroponics and heliostats (sunlight tracking mirrors)—plants are grown all around the building to provide organic shading, and direct sunlight is harvested all year long for heating and lighting. The shading saves cooling energy, while the redirected sunlight is an all-year light source for the building precinct and adjoining park.

Design Concept

OCP is the iconic centerpiece of the redevelopmen, supporting the underlying master plan assumption that Sydney's best locations for vertical living are near major inner city traffic nodes. More importantly though, by lifting the building mass off the ground and concentrating it along Broadway, space is released for a new public park.

The first design challenge is to give this pivotal new park a real presence at an urban scale. Because OCP is a high rise, it is possible to bring the park up into the sky along its facades and make it visible in the city at a distance. On the south side, the park rises in a sequence of planted plateaus that are scattered like puzzle pieces in randomized patterns across the facades, so that each apartment has not only a balcony, but also its own piece of the park. At the individual scale this creates pleasant private gardens and at a collective scale, a green urban sculpture. In this way, the building offers a flower to each resident and a bouquet to the city.

The second design challenge arises from the tall massing along the north side of the site. In order to remediate overshadowing of the park, the volume is broken up into a lower and a taller tower. On the roof of the lower tower, 42 heliostats redirect sunlight up to 320 reflectors on a cantilever off the taller tower, which then beam the light down into areas that would otherwise be in permanent shade. The system adapts hourly and seasonally to the need for brightness and warmth, so that the dappled lights move on the ground in a precisely programmed choreography. At night, the heliostat becomes a monumental urban chandelier and appears in the dark sky like a floating pool of tiny LED lights that merge into a giant screen and simulate reflections of glittering harbour waters.

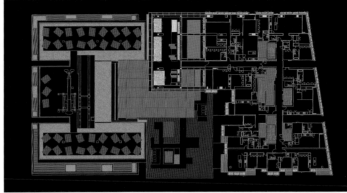
Level 29

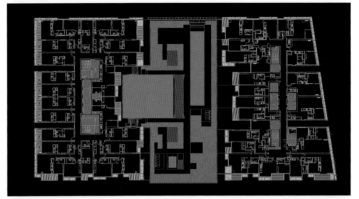
Level 6

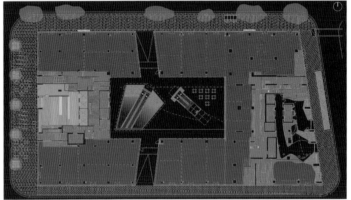
Level 0 S=1:1200

Sustainable Strategies

Four Strategies to Help Improve Sydney's Carbon Footprint:

1. Urban Density: OCP creates apartments where they're really needed: near the city's main job market in the nearby central business district. Sydney's population will grow by 4,000 new inhabitants per month, and residential towers near transportation nodes are a more sustainable development response than suburban sprawl of Sydney's Inner Western Suburbs.

2. Green Star: OCP improves the usually poor energy performance of residential high rises to meet a rating of at least five under the Australian Green Star standards and achieve a 25% reduction in energy consumption compared to the average.

3. Green Shading: improve energy performance with a system of 5 km long linear slab edge planters that function like permanent shading shelves and reduce thermal impact in the apartments by up to 30%. The plants are irrigated with recycled grey and black water, and their growth can be custom tailored to the needs of each facade area. During the intermediate seasons, the 2 m large glass sliding doors can be fully opened to benefit from the full impact of direct solar heat.

4. Green Energy: in addition to its TriGen Power Plant, OCP feature a system of solar power. 42 heliostats on the lower tower reflect direct sunlight up to 320 reflectors on a cantilever off the taller tower, which then beam the light down into an atrium, onto a pool deck and into the park. Water on the atrium glass roof absorbs the heat in the summer, but can be drained in the winter, so that the sunlight can help heat the space below. The heliostat system adapts hourly and seasonally to the needs for brightness and warmth in each place by shifting the light where it is the most useful. The cantilevered reflector shades the East Tower facade, while the heliostats on the West Tower massively reduce heat loads to the roof. The system redirects up to 200 m^2 of direct sunlight and utilizes approximately 40% of the corresponding power during Sydney's 2,600 annual sunshine hours. The performance of this system is not accounted for in the BASIX and Green Star calculations.

Elevation details with vegetation
植栽された壁面ディテール

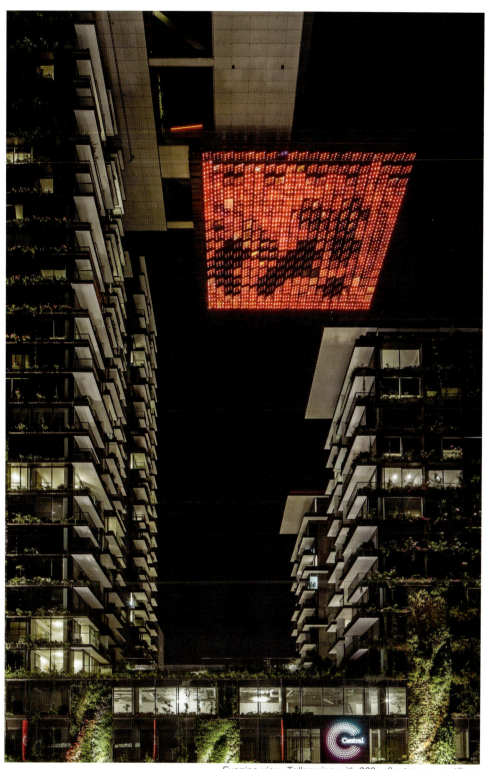

Evening view. Taller wing with 320 reflectors on cantilever
夕景。高層棟のキャンチレバーには320枚の反射板が取り付けられている

East wing (taller wing): view toward entrance
東棟（高層棟）：エントランスを見る

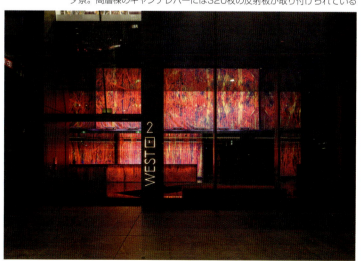

West wing (lower wing): entrance hall　西棟（低層棟）：エントランス・ホール

Roof terrace　ルーフテラス

View toward roof terrace through glazed walls　ガラス壁越しにルーフ・テラスを見る

Retail area. Escalator hall with vegetation　商業エリア：植栽されたエスカレータ・ホール

　ワン・セントラル・パーク（OCP）はフレイザーズ社と積水ハウスの取り組みによる革新的かつ環境に配慮したランドマークの計画である。敷地はシドニー・セントラル駅に程近く，カールトン＆ユナイテッド・ブルワリーズ醸造所の再開発計画として位置づけられている。全体計画はオーストラリアのグリーンスター環境評価基準に基づくもので，最上級のサステイナブルな居住空間の追求を目標に掲げ，環境に責任ある未来のまちづくりの展望への貢献をミッションとしたものである。現在，環境評価基準は単に取得するのみでは十分とは言えない傾向にある。ここではOCPの2棟の高層建築を緑化するために，設計は，グリーンスター評価制度の要求以上に炭素排出量を強く意識した広範囲なアプローチが採用された。計画では独自に2種類の技術——水耕栽培とヘリオスタット（集光ミラー）——が導入された。植物は建築のあらゆる場所に繁茂して木陰をつくる。ヘリオスタットは冷暖房と照明の負荷低減のため，常に太陽光の集光を行っている。木陰は冷房負荷を抑え，太陽光の反射は1年を通して建築と隣接する公園の光源として利用される。

設計のコンセプト
　OCPはこの再開発計画を象徴する中心的存在である。マスタープランによると，シドニー市街中心部の主要交通拠点の周辺は，高層建築の集住に相応しい地区に指定されていた。ここではさらに，垂直方向へ建築と地上を遊離し，ブロードウェイに集約することによって，パブリックスペースを公園として開放することに重点が置かれている。
　設計の第1段階では，中心となるこの新しい公園に，いかにして現実の都市スケールを付与するかが課題となった。OCPは高層建築である。そのため，公園をファサードに沿って空中高くへと引き上げることで，遠方からも視認させることが可能であった。南側は，ファサードを横断して，パズルのピースのようにランダムに散りばめられた植栽の台地のシークエンスとして公園が続く。そのため，各住戸はバルコニーに加え，公園の一部を自己の空間に取り入れることができる。緑は各住戸では快適なプライベート・ガーデン，集合住宅としては都市的スケールの彫刻となる。住民には一輪の花を，都市に対しては花束をこの建築はもたらしてくれる。
　設計の第2のポイントは敷地北側にそびえるマッスに由来するものである。公園への日影を改善するため，ヴォリュームは低層棟と高層棟に分割された。低層棟の屋上には42枚のヘリオスタットが，高層棟のキャンチレバーには320枚の反射板が取り付けられている。低層棟の光は高層棟で再反射することで，永久日影となる区画に光を照射する役割を果たす。このシステムは必要な照度と

温度に対し，常に最適化されている。そのため，まだら模様の光の跡はプログラムによって正確な軌跡を地表に描く。日が落ちるとヘリオスタットはこの都市を象徴するシャンデリアとして，暗闇へと浮遊する。港で水面が反射して煌めくように，この小さなLEDの光のプールは，巨大なスクリーンに溶け込んでゆく。

サステイナブルな方法論
シドニーの炭素排出量を抑制する4本の柱
1．都市の集密度：必要とされる地域に集合住宅を供給すること。商業地域の中心に位置する主要労働市場への近接性。シドニーの人口は毎月4,000人ずつ増加する見込みである。交通拠点に隣接したレジデンシャル・タワーは，シドニーのインナー・ウェスタン地区における郊外のスプロール化と比較して，一層サステイナブルな開発計画となっている。
2．グリーンスター：高層集合住宅に見られる非効率的なエネルギー消費の改善。オーストラリア・グリーンスター環境評価制度において，少なくともファイブ・スターを取得することにより，平均と比較して25％のエネルギー消費の低減を図る。
3．グリーン・シェーディング：プランターによるエネルギー効率の向上。全長5キロにわたりスラブ端部へと取り付けられたプランターは恒久的なライトシェルフとして機能する。住戸への熱負荷は最大30％低減される。植物は再生水と生活水を利用した灌漑によって育てられ，個々のファサードには必要に応じて植栽が施される予定。中間期には直接光の熱を十分に享受するため，2メートルの巨大なガラスのスライド・ドアを完全に開放することができる。
4．グリーンエネルギー：トリジェネレーションによる発電施設と太陽光エネルギーシステム。低層棟の42枚のヘリオスタットと，高層棟キャンチレバーの320枚の反射板。太陽光は低層棟から高層棟へと反射し，光線はその下のアトリウムやプールサイド，公園へと再反射する。夏期にはアトリウムの屋根のガラスの水が熱を吸収すると共に，冬期には水を抜き，太陽の光で下部の空間を暖めることができる。ヘリオスタットは年間を通して常に，各々の場所に必要な照度と温度に合わせて，光の向きを変えることができる。キャンチレバーの反射板は東棟のファサードに日影をつくり，西棟のヘリオスタットは屋根面の熱負荷を大幅に低減する。このシステムでは200平米の太陽光を再反射させることにより，2,600時間のシドニーの日照時間の約40％に等しいエネルギーを利用することが可能となった。これはBASIXやグリーンスターの評価手法とは異なる省エネルギーシステムである。

Upward view of taller wing　高層棟見上げ

View from Central Park on southwest　南西側セントラル・パークより見る

2009–11
SANAA

SHAKUJII APARTMENT
Tokyo, Japan

A Versatile Environment of Small Shifts

The project is an eight-unit, row house-style apartment complex located in a quiet residential district lined with low-rise homes. Instead of building an extensive volume within a neighborhood of single-family houses, the apartment is designed by slightly shifting room-sized volumes on the horizontal and vertical axis. Each volume is simply structured using columns and slabs of different levels. The apartment consists of roofed terraces and parking lots, and a host of uniquely designed units: some expand horizontally, some have rooms that continue vertically, and some are half underground with a relaxing ambience. By incorporating the gardens, terraces, and parking spaces into the arrangement of the apartment units, the entire complex becomes a highly concentrated building with varying depths. The spaces throughout the complex are characterized by a bright and airy ambience, as if the outdoors have been mixed into the indoors.

Shifts in small scales create variations in the relationships between not only the rooms themselves, but between outdoors and indoors, and among the inhabitants. An accumulation of these small, shifting relationships creates a building that is versatile and flexible as a whole. My goal was to create a versatile environment that loosely follows the surrounding scenery, while inspiring various relationships with the neighborhood.

Site plan S=1:2400

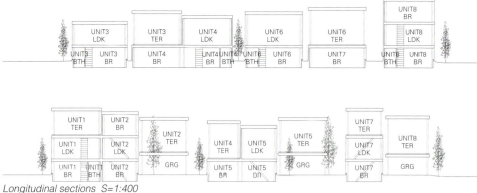

Longitudinal sections S=1:400

South elevation 南面

Overall view from southeast　南東側全景

View from entrance of unit 5. Terrace of unit 5 (right) and terrace of unit 6 (left)　住戸5の玄関より庭を見る。右は住戸5のテラス、左は住戸6のテラス

小さなズレがつくるやわらかな環境

低層な家々が広がる閑静な住宅街に位置する全8世帯の長屋形式の集合住宅である。周囲は戸建てサイズのヴォリュームが立っている中，長大なヴォリュームを避け，部屋サイズのヴォリュームを平面，断面方向に小さくずらしながら配置した。各ヴォリュームは柱とスラブのシンプルな構造を持ち，様々なレベルのスラブを実現し，住戸は平面的に広がった部屋や，断面方向に続く居室，半地下の落ち着いた部屋の他に，屋根付きのテラスや駐車場で構成されている。庭やテラス，駐車場も部屋と一緒に並べることで，高密度だけれども明るく風通しがよく様々な奥行きを持つ建物となり，屋外と屋内が混ざり合ったような空間が建物全体に広がっている。

小さなスケールでのずれが部屋と部屋との関係性だけではなく屋外や屋内との関係性，住む人びととの関係性を多様なものとし，それらが集まることによってできる全体としてのひとつのやわらかな建物のかたちが表れた。周辺の街に様々な関係性をつくりだしながら，街にゆるやかに連続しつつ，やわらかな環境をつくり出せるよう目指した。

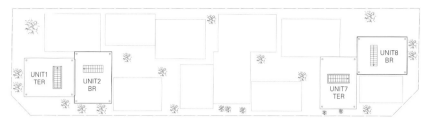

Third floor

Second floor

First floor S=1:400

Cross sections

BR BEDROOM
BTH BATHROOM
GRG GARAGE
LDK LIVING ROOM/DINING ROOM/KITCHEN
TER TERRACE

Unit 7: bedroom on basement　住戸7：地階寝室

Unit 6: living room/dining room on second floor　住戸6：2階居間／食堂

Looking west from terrace of unit 7 住戸7のテラスより西を見る

Looking north from terrace of unit 6 toward unit 5 住戸6のテラスより北の住戸5を見る

2010–13
KAZUYO SEJIMA

KYOTO APARTMENTS (NISHINOYAMA HOUSE)
Kyoto, Japan

Overall view from north　北側全景

Aerial view from east　東側上空より見る

Site plan　S=1:5000

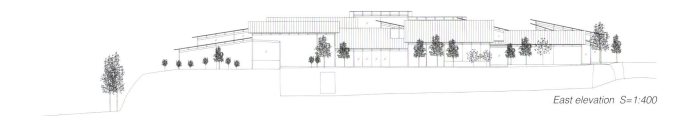

East elevation S=1:400

View from east: common terrace on left   東より見る。左側は共有テラス △▽

Unit 3: evening view 住戸3：夕景

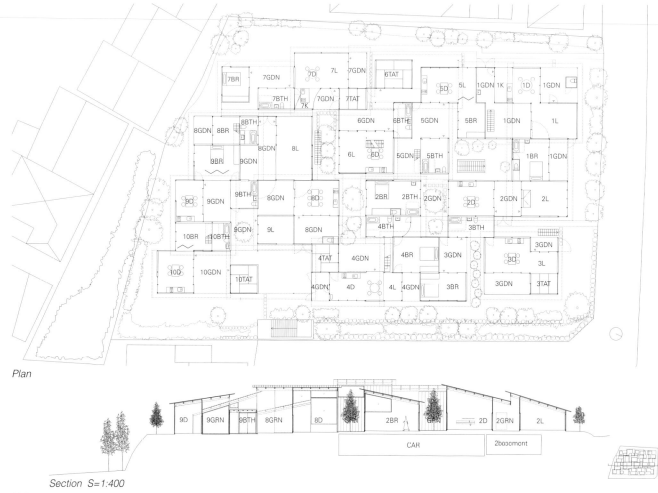

Plan

Section S=1:400

Unit 5: dining room/kitchen　住戸5：食堂／台所

Unit 5: garden view from bathroom　住戸5：浴室から庭を見る

The project is a ten-unit rental housing complex in a quiet residential area in Kyoto. The complex is built on a gently sloping site with a distant view of the Kyoto city and Mount Hiei. According to the city's regulations, projects of this area are required to follow the local landscape, including roof design, colors and materials used.

Instead of enveloping the entire complex with one large roof, we chose to design twenty-one separate roofs with similar sizes as those of the surrounding buildings. We took each room, as opposed to each unit, and covered them with different roofs to create a mixed cluster that amount to a large connective roof of the entire complex.

Each unit is sized around fifty-five to a hundred square meters, consisting of three to four rooms with either a loft or a basement. These units contain three different roofs, one of which is connected to another unit. This results in an assortment of unique floor-plans that are connected by a large roof, a concept that is distinctly different from a community of single-family homes. Spaces are positioned on different levels according to the site elevation, and the gradient, direction, and height of the roofs are also diversified to generate vertical changes in the expansion and illumination of the spaces.

As if one is pushing through an entangled space, the complex stands as an ambiguous and unpredictable amalgamation of public/private, and indoors/outdoors, where a living room might be standing in one corner, a sun-drenched bathroom in another; a shady deck and an alleyway lead to the neighboring inner gardens and backyards, and a common courtyard appears between the roofs.

The variance in the design's spatial composition promotes a sense of excitement and the fun of living in this complex. We hope that this vibrant spirit will emanate towards the surrounding environment to create a uniquely fertile environment and a harmonious panorama.

Takashige Yamashita/Kazuyo Sejima & Associates

京都の閑静な住宅地に建つ，10戸からなる賃貸の集合住宅である。敷地は遠くに比叡山や京都の町並みを一望できるなだらかな丘陵地にある。京都市の規制により，屋根形状や色彩，素材への配慮と，町並みとの調和がとれた計画がこの地域一帯の建物には求められる。

私たちは，1棟の建物にそのまま大きな屋根を架けるのではなく，周りの建物に近い大きさの21枚の屋根を，住戸単位というよりは部屋単位に架けていき，バラバラな屋根の集まりによって一つの大屋根が感じられるような集合住宅をつくろうと考えた。

各住戸は55～100平米程度で，三つから四つの部屋とロフトまたは地下で組み合わされるが，1住戸には3枚の屋根があり，そのうちの1枚の屋根が他の住戸にまたがっているため，戸建て住宅が単に集合するのとは異なるさまざまなプランがひとつ屋根の下に広がっている。また，敷地の高低差に合わせて少しずつ段差をつけて全体を配置し，さらに屋根の勾配や方向，高さも変えているため，光の入り方や空間の広がりなど，断面的にも変化が生まれている。

分け入っていくような空間のつながり方の中で，たまたまそこにリビングがあって，サンルームのお風呂があり，木陰の縁側，お隣の坪庭や裏庭へと続く路地，屋根の切れ間にあらわれるみんなの中庭など，屋内と屋外，パブリックとプライベートが偶然混ざり合ったような割り切れない関係で全体が成り立っている。

どこをとっても違う展開を見せる空間構成は，ここに住んだら楽しいという気持ちを湧き立たせてくれる。そのいきいきとした感じが，屋内外だけでなく周辺ともつながって，集まるからこそ生まれる豊かな環境と良好な景観を築き上げられたらと思っている。

（山下貴成／妹島和世建築設計事務所）

Common terrace between unit 9 and 10: court of unit 8 on left　住戸9と住戸10の間の共有テラス：左奥に住戸8の庭

Unit 10: bedroom　住戸10：寝室

Unit 9　住戸9

Unit 6　住戸6

Court of unit 2: looking east 住戸2の庭：東を見る

View toward unit 1 through common court from unit 2 住戸2より共有の庭を介して住戸1を見る

Unit 2: court connecting bathroom and dining/kitchen 住戸2：庭を介して浴室と食堂／台所がつながる

Acknowledgements

Copyright of Drawings:
All drawings are provided by the architects except as noted.
- © FLC/ADAGP, Paris & JASPAR, Tokyo, 2014 D0921: pp.10-11
- "Mies van der Rohe—The Art of Structure"
  edited by Werner Blaser, Thames and Hudson: p.16

Copyright of Photographs:
- © Tomio Ohashi: p.62 bottom
- © Gehry Partners, LLP: p.221 bottom left
- © Kazuyo Sejima & Associates: p.264 bottom

English translation:
Satoko Hirata, Erica Sakai, and others

Japanese translation:
Yasuko Kikuchi, Masayuki Harada, and others

GA現代建築シリーズ13
〈集合住宅1〉

2015年1月23日発行

```
     企画              二川幸夫
     編集              二川由夫
     撮影              GA photographers
ロゴタイプ・デザイン      細谷巖
    発行者             二川由夫
   印刷・製本           図書印刷株式会社
     発行              エーディーエー・エディタ・トーキョー
                      東京都渋谷区千駄ヶ谷3-12-14
                      TEL.(03) 3403-1581(代)
```

禁無断転載

ISBN 978-4-87140-583-6 C1352